10/04

I Need Help With School!

by

Becky Moyes

I NEED HELP WITH SCHOOL!

All marketing and publishing rights guaranteed to and reserved by

721 W. Abram Street

Arlington, Texas 76013

800-489-0727

817-277-0727

817-277-2270 (fax)

E-mail: info@futurehorizons-autism.com

www.FutureHorizons-autism.com

Cataloging in Publications Data is available from the Library of Congress.

ISBN   1-885477-98-8

ACKNOWLEDGEMENTS

For Clenise Vincent, Georgiann Landowski, Jennifer Seminuk
and Mary Limbacher—the most persistent and effective team members I know!

For Mrs. Shannon Wagner, a middle school principal with conviction and heart.

For special friends like Anna Scott, Ronna Hochbein, Marla Green and Cindy
Waeltermann who get the job done for other parents as well.

And . . . .

For Chuck,
my wonderful and supportive husband:

This one's finally for you!

TABLE OF CONTENTS

Chapter One

To Tell or Not to Tell

When parents receive the diagnosis of any autism spectrum disorder for their child, they often wrestle with the decision of whether or not to share this information with their child's school district officials. This is particularly true with the diagnosis of autism/Asperger's syndrome.

Children with autism/Asperger's often present to the world as typical children: they look more similar to their peers than not; they participate in their home and community; they have no identifying physical features and are often bright and articulate. It is often only upon closer inspection (and usually in social situations) that their deficits become truly evident.

As a parent of a child with autism/Asperger's and as a consultant/advocate for this population, the author has seen the "to tell or not to tell" dilemma present itself more often than not. Parents hope that with early treatment and/or diagnosis, their child will become indistinguishable from their peers and will not require special education services in the school setting. They sometimes feel that labeling their child as a special needs student may place an unnecessary burden on them that they may have to carry throughout their lifetime. Parents worry that labeling the child may also cause their placement to change, and then the entire school will learn that they are a special education student.

Unfortunately, children with autism/Asperger's rarely become totally indistinguishable from their peers because of the very nature of this social behavioral disability. Parents, (and some school professionals) need to understand that this is not a personality "quirk"; it is a life-time disability. Therefore, to some extent, this child will have some symptoms ranging from mild to severe throughout their school years and into their adult life. There will always be moments socially and emotionally that will challenge or frustrate them. Our goal as parents and educators is to help this child reach their maximum potential. This is done by providing the necessary supports and specially designed instruction that is needed at each level of development. Unfortunately, in today's school system, this can only be accomplished by recognizing the child as a special needs student through a formal evaluation or identification process.

Mary and Dennis received their son's diagnosis of Asperger's syndrome when he was a three-year old. The therapist that worked with their child urged them to refrain from involving early intervention specialists in the school system, explaining that it was their hope that by the time he entered kindergarten, he would no longer meet the criteria for this diagnosis, and the school would not need to know about his disability. At the age of five, Mary enrolled Michael in his local school kindergarten. It was her desire to have someone in the school environment facilitate Michael's social skills development during recess, but this could not be accomplished by his child's teacher as she took her lunch period during recess. About two months after school began, Michael began to exhibit problem behaviors as a result of his lack of support services. Because he was not yet identified as a special needs student, Michael received no behavioral supports for his disability until he was tested by the district (a process that took sixty school days) and an individualized education plan (IEP) developed. During that period, he was afforded the same disciplinary actions as typical students for his problem behaviors.

As this example also shows, the earlier the school can be involved in the process of making accommodations for the social needs of the student, the better. Consider the following as well:

Example II:

Joshua was twelve when an astute psychologist diagnosed him with Asperger's syndrome. In his preschool years, Joshua was delayed in his language development and rarely interacted with his peers. In his elementary years, his odd behaviors, mannerisms and restricted interests isolated him from his classmates and caused him to be the brunt of teasing. Many school meetings were held with Joshua's parents to develop a "game plan" for helping Joshua to fit in better, but none of these meetings considered the fact that Joshua needed to learn social skills in a different way than his peers. Fortunately for Joshua, his grades did not suffer during this time. After obtaining the diagnosis, his thankful parents then shared the report with their school, and special education testing was initiated by the district. Because Joshua was not demonstrating a need for academic help, the district could not qualify him under special education regulations but agreed to provide him with social supports and accommodations via a Chapter 15 service agreement.[1]

As you can see by the above two examples, it would have been much easier for the children involved if the disability had been identified early in their school years, and/or if the information had then been promptly shared with the district. Schools that are able to follow the development and progress of these children at an early age tend to become very familiar with the child's needs and make-up. Precious time is not wasted convincing school staff to agree to services the parents feel their child requires.

Parents should ask two very important questions when making the decision whether or not to share with the school their child's diagnosis:

---

[1] Chapter 15 Service Agreement, Rehabilitation Act, Section 504. Published at 29 U.S.C. Section 794 and the implementing regulations at 34 C.F.R. Part 104.

1. Does my child need added supports that are different from those that his peers require because of his academic, social or behavioral challenges?

2. Are having those supports more important to them than having a label?

Parents need to understand that classroom polices, rules and procedures (including discipline, academic assistance provided, etc.) are basically the same for all children who are typical. Changes and modifications to the classroom environment or curriculum do not usually happen unless children are identified. That means your child's behavioral differences will not be considered as manifestations of their disability unless he/she has been formally recognized by your school district as a special needs student.

Phillip, a child with Asperger's, was prone to angry outbursts when he became sensory overloaded. His parents had not shared Phillip's diagnosis of Asperger's syndrome with the district. Phillip would frequently lose his recess time for inadequate class work. He often used the swings during this period to help him to unwind. Without this physical outlet, his stress increased in the afternoons, often resulting in a display of even more aggressive-type behaviors with peers. As Phillip continued to receive more consequences for his behavior, his self-esteem began to drop. He became clinically depressed and required medication.

In the case of Phillip above, an outside observer could easily see that had Phillip been provided with a solid behavior support plan that included mechanisms to prevent sensory overload, his spiral into depression and the resulting need for medication may have been avoided. The protections in this case were clearly more important to this child than the "Exceptional Student" label he would receive had he been identified.

In conclusion, the author would like to provide a measure of comfort to those who struggle with the idea of informing their school districts about their child's disability. Special education law is very clear about protecting the confidentiality rights of special needs children.

There is truly no need for classmates and others students to know the content of a child's individualized education program or the type of services being provided.

Although all school staff who interact with the student should be informed of the student's needs, the support they are to provide is to be kept confidential from peers, staff who do not interact with the student and other parents. These rights are protected by both the state and federal governments.[2]

[2]Rehabilitation Act, Section 504. Published at 29 U.S.C. Section 794 and the implementing regulations at 34 C.F.R. Part 104.

Chapter Two

Taking the First Step

After parents receive their evaluation report from their diagnosing professional, it is advised by the author that they share the results with their school district. In order for the district to provide special education services, parents will need to request that the district conduct their own evaluation for special education services, utilizing the diagnosing report as a guideline. This should always be done in writing with a dated letter.

(See Figure 2.1 pg. 14)

School districts do not have to accept outside testing results but must consider those results in decision-making for your child. The credentials of the diagnosing doctor are important, with recommendations made by certified school psychologists in your state carrying more weight. Medical doctors (such as pediatricians, neurologists or psychiatrists) often diagnose these children and make educational recommendations for students. However, their reports should be signed-off by psychologists so that their recommendations carry more weight with school districts. Parents may want to check their doctor's credentials before making their appointments for independent testing. If the initial diagnosing doctor recommends other evaluations for your child (ex.: speech, occupational

December 5, 2003

Dr. Joseph Carleton
Special Education Director
Riverside School District
300 Moravia Street
Brookville, OH 43561

Dear Dr. Carleton:

We would like to request a multi-disciplinary evaluation for our son, Robert Reynolds, who is a third-grade student at Brookside Elementary School.

Robert was recently diagnosed with Asperger's Syndrome, a Pervasive Developmental Disorder. We are enclosing a copy of Dr. Luca's diagnosing report. Dr. Lucas also felt that our child has a central auditory processing disorder. In addition to testing for the presence of a learning disability, we would like the district to conduct a full language assessment to evaluate his auditory processing ability as well as his social language/social skill deficits.

We will be looking forward to receiving parent input forms so that we can provide a more detailed summary of our concerns.

This letter serves as our permission to begin the evaluation process.

Sincerely yours,
Frederick Reynolds
Marlene Reynolds

Figure 2.1

therapy), these should also be completed and reports obtained before approaching your school district with the results. The more thorough your own testing, the less likely the school district will refrain from providing needed services.

Once the district receives your letter requesting a special education evaluation, they should send you parent input forms and a permission form to begin the testing. The parent input forms are used so that you can share with the district the concerns you have about your child in a formal way. This input will eventually find its way into the district's evaluation report that they will produce at the conclusion of their testing to determine your child's eligibility. You want to be sure to write specific details about your concerns. If you have samples of school work that show where your child is having trouble, include copies of these as well. If the questions on the input form do not tease out the concerns you have, draw an arrow at the bottom of the form and write on the back or include an attachment adding the words "attachment included" in a prominent location on the form. Provide a copy of your outside testing results to the district. Excerpts from all of the outside testing results will also find their way into the concluding report.

After the district receives your signed permission form, testing can then be initiated, and the timelines for the process will begin. (You should check with educational advocates in your particular state concerning how quickly the evaluation must be completed, and a report issued to you. You should be aware that in some states, the evaluation process can take up to sixty school days so that a process that begins at the end of May, for instance, may not be concluded until October of the next school year.)

Always Keep a Copy!

Example I:

Toni and Dave initiated testing for special education with their school district for their newly-diagnosed child. When the concluding report was presented, Toni felt very little of their parent input was included in the report. Toni and Dave had not kept a copy of their parent input sheet and were too embarrassed to ask the district if they had kept the form in their file.

Keeping good records is important! Parents should make copies of the documents that they have completed and every letter or evaluation report they share with the district. They should begin a file folder of these documents as they pertain to each school year.

The Evaluation Report

Once the district has finished its own evaluation, it will issue an Evaluation Report (ER) to you. Sometimes this report is mailed to you, and sometimes it is presented in person. In all cases, you should have an opportunity to meet and discuss the findings with the district. Very often, there may be several people present at this meeting including the school psychologist, the principal and possibly your child's teacher. Sometimes, however, the report is presented by the school psychologist in a private meeting with you.

After you have had a chance to review the document (and it is recommended that you take the document home and think about it and compare it to the findings of your independent evaluators), you will have the opportunity to state whether you agree with the findings of the report or whether you disagree.

You should pay close attention to the "Conclusions" or "Summary" section of the document, as this will detail whether your child is found eligible for special education services or not.

If you agree with the findings of the report, your district may ask you to sign that you agree, and they will then:

- Make arrangements for an IEP (Individualized Education Plan) meeting if your child is eligible for special education.

- Make arrangements for a Section 504 Service Agreement meeting if your child is not eligible for special education but requires accommodations as a disabled student (more about this in the next chapter).

- Find your child ineligible for any of the above.

If you do not agree with the findings of the report, you should detail the reasons why you do not agree in a letter, being as specific as possible. Generally, the reasons why parents object to the findings of a report center around several basic areas:

1. The instruments that were used to evaluate the child were not appropriate for what they were intended to measure.

Example II:

Terry was a child who was diagnosed with Asperger's and Attention Deficit Hyperactivity Disorder-Inattentive Type (ADHD). The district evaluated Terry's attention issues using the short-form of a rating scale that was primarily used to measure maladaptive-type behaviors sometimes associated with ADHD. Terry did not display such problems in the classroom or at home. Consequently, the results of the scale were interpreted by the district as demonstrating that Terry did not display symptoms in the school environment for ADHD-Inattentive Type. Terry was found ineligible for services. When Terry's parents presented the report to the diagnosing doctor and asked why there was such a discrepancy between the doctor's diagnosis and the district's findings, the doctor explained that the scale the district had used was not an appropriate tool to measure ADHD-Inattentive Type.

2.   The evaluation was not comprehensive (it did not include tests to measure all aspects of the child's suspected disability).

Example III:

David was a child who exhibited many social problems in the school environment. His parents felt that he was not able to carry on appropriate conversations, initiate greetings or maintain the topic of conversation. They requested a multi-disciplinary evaluation and expressed many concerns about their child's progress in this area on their parent input form. No evaluations, however, were conducted to evaluate David's social skills, other than an observation of David in the classroom which detailed that David raised his hand to participate and worked quietly at his seat and did not interfere with the proceedings of the classroom.

All aspects of the child's suspected disability must be tested. The suspected disability information comes from your parent input form, your independent evaluation reports and also information collected from school staff.

3. Parent input/private evaluations were not included, input from present classroom teachers or observations was not obtained.

One evaluation report included excerpts from comments of a student's art and music teacher (in whose class the child was not having problems) but failed to gather information from his classroom teacher who had tremendous concerns about the student.

If you feel that the evaluation was not complete or not representative of your child because of any of the above, you can request that the district continue to evaluate and gather additional information. You should state your reasons why in a letter to the district.

If it is apparent that the report is not at all an accurate representation of your child or the district refuses to continue gathering data, you may also request an independent evaluation at public expense. A list of evaluators will be presented to you, and you will have the opportunity to begin the process again with a new evaluator. If the district feels that their evaluation was sufficient; however, they may not agree to pay for the evaluation. If the district does not agree to pay for the evaluation, they must then notify you of their decision in writing and provide you with an opportunity to challenge this through a pre-hearing conference, mediation or a due process hearing. If parents want to avoid the costs associated with a due process hearing, asking for a continuation of the evaluation process to gather missing data may be the best route.

Parents that find themselves in the quandary about whether or not to accept the findings of the district but want to avoid a due process hearing should realize that the evaluation report is the blueprint of services for their child. If the evaluation report does not outline sufficiently the services that your child needs or does not conclude the need of services at all, the author recommends that you write a letter to the district stating concisely what is wrong with the evaluation report and what you would like to have changed. Consider this report to be a draft and that it is a work-in-progress that can be amended.

If presented a signature page requesting your approval, it is important to check "I disagree," if that is the case. In this event, you should include a notation that your dissenting letter is attached. If you are not presented with any sign-off sheet where you can mark that you disagree, you should still send your dissenting letter. Other team members who participated in the evaluation will also have the chance to agree or disagree with the findings. You should make a mental note of the signatures that were included on this page, particularly if some of the individuals listed have previously voiced concerns to you about your child's progress but then signed that they agree with the report. In your dissenting letter, it might be helpful to state that those particular individuals have spoken to you previously about their concerns, and you are confused as to why they now feel the child does not need specially designed instruction.

If they disagree with the findings it is wise for parents to request a meeting in writing to discuss their dissenting letter with district officials. In this way, they may be able to avoid the expense of a due process hearing. If there are school staff who seem to support your view point or who also have concerns regarding your child's progress, ask that they also be present at the meeting. If they have agreed with the findings of the report on the sign-off sheet ask why. Share some of the child's work. Reiterate the findings of the private evaluator.

Eligibility for Special Education Services

A determination for eligibility for an IEP is based on two prongs:

1. That the child is a child with a disability.

2. That the child is in need of specially designed instruction (instruction that is unique and is tailored to address that particular student's style of learning).

A child who is making "A"'s and "B"'s on their report card, or whose classroom performance is average or above will probably not be found eligible because of the second-prong requirement. However, a child who has an IQ in the superior range (120+) and is making "C"'s on their report card may be considered eligible because he is working substantially below their ability level and possibly needs special education to address their unique style of learning so that they can work up to their potential. If there is a significant discrepancy (15 points or more) between the performance IQ and the verbal IQ score, or a great discrepancy between some of the individual subtest standard scores in the evaluation report, the child may be found eligible because of a particular learning disability (for instance in reading or math), in addition to the autism/Asperger's syndrome if their grades or classroom performance are suffering.

Example V:

Ralph was an elementary student diagnosed with Asperger's at the beginning of third grade. His school district evaluated him and found his IQ to be in the average range. However, on some of the subtests of the IQ test used by the district, Ralph's scores ranged from a two in reading comprehension to a ten in block assembly. The district found Ralph eligible for special education because of the significant discrepancy on several of his subtests and because he seemed to be having a problem with reading in the classroom. He was determined eligible for an IEP based on his Asperger's diagnosis and also as a learning disabled child in the area of reading.

If the classroom performance does not indicate that the child is suffering academically, however, he may be disqualified for services despite his diagnosis. (A special note of interest: grades should not be used as the sole-determinant for eligibility as they are only subjective measures of performance.)

Example VI:

Rick has Asperger's syndrome and his behavior is often very difficult in the classroom. His teacher is often frustrated because he talks out, becomes angry, refuses to do work and is sometimes aggressive towards his peers. His grades are in the average range and appropriate for a child with average intelligence. Rick's classroom performance, however, should qualify him for special education services because of his disability and his need for specially designed instruction to teach him to focus and be more appropriate socially.

As was stated previously, a child with a disability that does not meet the second-prong requirement above can also be eligible for accommodations in the classroom if the disability impacts on a major life function. For children with autism/Asperger's, the disability certainly impacts on the student's social skills,

communication, behavior, etc. These children should not have problems

qualifying under Section 504 of the Rehabilitation Act and be provided a Chapter

15 Service Agreement if the evaluation report shows documentation of the above

impacting in the school setting.

Example VII:

Andy was a fourth-grade student who received his diagnosis of

Asperger's syndrome by an out-of-district psychologist. He was having

difficulty with social skills and managing anxiety in the classroom.

When the district conducted their own evaluation, they found Andy to

have a low average IQ. Although he was making "C's" and "D's" on his

report card, he was not found eligible for special education services

because his performance was not significantly discrepant from his

ability (IQ score). Andy was found eligible, however, for a 504 Service

Agreement because the district acknowledged Andy's difficulties in

the classroom because of his Asperger's syndrome.

Summary

The process of determining eligibility for special education services in school age children is two-pronged and can be lengthy and confusing. Children with autism/Asperger's fall under the Pervasive Developmental Disorders category of eligibility. However, these children may or may not qualify as a student who needs special education services (IEP's) if they are found not to be in need of specially designed instruction.

If the district conducts a multi-disciplinary evaluation and determines a child to be ineligible for special education and the parents disagree, the parents can then request that the district pay for an independent evaluation. Parent who are dissenting the findings of an evaluation report can feel comfortable requesting an independent evaluation and/or winning a due process hearing if they feel one of the following conditions exist:

- The child's suspected disability was not evaluated.

- The child's evaluation was not inclusive (ex: if your parent input or private evaluation reports indicated social skills problems or auditory processing concerns and no such test was provided).

- Appropriate testing tools were not used. (Tests were used that did not measure what they were intended to measure.)

- One single test was used as a determining factor for eligibility and other data was ignored.

- Your child's teachers did not provide input.

- Your parent input was not included.

- Your private evaluations were not considered.

- School-based observations of your child's behavior were not included.

- The tests were not conducted under standard conditions. (The child was tested in a noisy room, when he was sick or hungry, or there were frequent interruptions during the testing process.)

If parents are not pleased with the findings of the report, they should make every effort to work these concerns out with the district and ask that the ER be revised. The evaluation (ER) report drives the services that your child will obtain. If you are not in agreement with this report, you will probably not be in agreement with the services the school will be providing to your child.

Although your child may not be found eligible for special education services, they are still a child with a disability who may require accommodations disability if it can be shown that the disability impacts on performance in any aspect of

school life (sensory processing, social skills, gross motor skills, fine motor skills)

through a 504 Service Agreement under Chapter 15 of the Rehabilitation Act.

Chapter Three

Section 504 Regulations

Since 1973, Section 504 of the Rehabilitation Act has played a significant part in assuring that children with disabilities receive appropriate accommodations. The Office of Civil Rights (OCR) oversees the enforcement of Section 504 and prohibits discrimination against individuals with handicaps in any programs or activities of any school district which receives federal funds. Section 504 requires that students with handicaps have equal opportunity to those programs and services that typical children may have access to.

Example I:

In one school district, the number of children had outgrown the building size and children with autism were confined to a classroom located in a trailer or "pod" outside the main school building. Parents of these children filed suit under OCR claiming that the classroom was smaller and substandard to that of the typical children's classrooms inside the main school building. OCR found the school district to be out of compliance and ordered them to eliminate the use of the trailer for the autistic classroom as it detached the special needs children from their typical classmates. "Pods" could be used for various other types of classes where children with disabilities were integrated, provided that such sites contained modifications for children with all types of disabilities (for instance, wheel-chair accessibility).

Every child who is identified and provided with an IEP under the Individuals with Disabilities Education Act (IDEA) is also protected under Section 504. As explained in Chapter Two, however, children identified under Section 504 may not be protected under IDEA because of the two-prong eligibility criteria. An easy way to distinguish between the two is to use the "disabled" and "handicapped" labels in a distinctive manner: those children who have met the two-prong eligibility criteria are found to be "disabled" and qualify for accommodations under IDEA (that is, an Individualized Education Program [IEP],) those children found to be "handicapped" but not in need of specially designed instruction qualify for accommodations under Section 504 (that is, a 504 Service Agreement).

If a child with autism/Asperger's does not qualify under IDEA, their district should consider if they need support under Section 504. School districts are under obligation to not only evaluate children suspected of having a handicap or disability brought to their attention by parents or teachers, but also to seek out and evaluate children who display certain characteristics that put them at-risk (ex. a child who is going to be retained, a child who takes medication administered at school for a health condition, a child who has severe behavior or social problems). The determination of eligibility for a Service Agreement is also done through an evaluation process by a group of people knowledgeable about the student's disability. For this reason a review of medical records is important.

Evaluations are used to determine what accommodations a child with a handicap might require in order for them to have full access to classroom and school activities and put them on 'a level playing field' with their nondisabled peers. For children with physical disabilities such as diabetes, accommodations might include that a school nurse would be available to check sugar levels or to administer orange juice as needed when insulin levels drop. Or, a child with juvenile arthritis, for instance, may need to have the use of a keyboard when writing tasks are painful. For children with autism/Asperger's, accommodations might include the use of a guidance counselor to help address social skills development or the use of a speech/language teacher to address pragmatic language skills. Just because a child with autism/Asperger's is making good grades in the classroom does not mean that he is not entitled to accommodations because of their disability.

Example II:

Julie was a 15-year old Asperger's student who was mentally gifted. She received a gifted IEP to address her need for academic acceleration and enrichment. The document did not address her social and emotional needs as a student with Asperger's. Her parents requested a 504 Service Agreement evaluation to address her handicap and to provide her with accommodations as there was much evidence that these deficits were impacting on her school day.

Types of Accommodations that May Be Utilized in a 504 Service Agreement

There may be a need to modify the classroom in several ways for children with autism/Asperger's:

- Allowing the student to move through the hallways prior to other students.

- Allowing the student to review changes to his/her schedule on a daily basis.

- Allowing the student to sit in close proximity to the teacher.

- Reducing stimuli.

- Allowing for a "cool-down" place or a "safe person."

- Removing a student with auditory sensitivities prior to a fire drill.

- Adjusting the length of time to complete tests, answer questions or record answers.

- Modifying homework assignments in length or increasing the time expected to complete them.

- Allowing the student to use computers or tape recorders.

- Allowing the use of visual or tactile teaching methods.

- Reducing the reading level of classroom materials.

Parents and teachers can create a Service Agreement that is every bit as effective as an IEP provided that it is specific and tailored to the child's needs. Parents should not insist that every accommodation that may be provided for children with autism/Asperger's be applied to their child's Service Agreement. Children are individuals and the length of the 504 Service Agreement is not what makes the document a sound one. Districts are completely liable for providing the provisions they agree to do in the document, and the document can be revisited at any time.

Qualifying a Child Under Section 504

A child should be a student identified as handicapped if they meet any of the following criteria:

1. Has a mental or physical impairment which substantially limits one or more major life activities (walking, seeing, breathing, talking, hearing, learning, working, etc.) or

2. Has a record of such an impairment (a diagnosis or doctor's report) or

3. Is regarded as having such an impairment (ex: is being treated by a doctor as someone who has this impairment)[1]

Districts need to be proactive in qualifying children under Section 504 or IDEA if they suspect the presence of a disability or handicap, or they can be found liable for discriminating against such children due to their failure to provide accommodations. If parents have requested a 504 evaluation and then later disagree with the findings of this evaluation or the accommodations the district is willing to provide, they can request mediation or an impartial due process hearing or file a local grievance with the Office of Civil Rights.

---

[1]"Student Access: A Resource Guide for Educators, Section 504 of the Rehabilitation Act of 1973," Council of Administrators of Special Education, Inc., Indiana University, Bloomington, IN 47405.

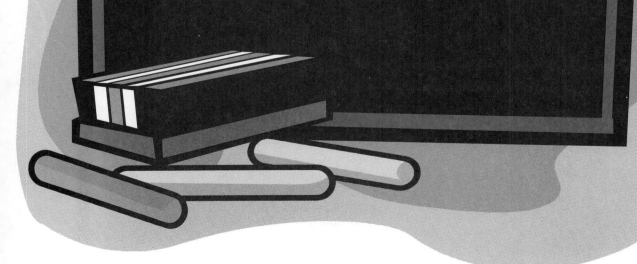

Chapter Four

Basic Advocacy 101

Guiding Star #1:
Realize that special education is a team process; be respectful of your role on that team.

Many parents do not realize that the process of special education is based on the team concept. A team decides whether a child is eligible for services, a team decides what services need to be provided to him/her, a team decides the contents of an IEP or 504 and a team evaluates whether the program devised is working.

Parents (and administrators) who have a good understanding of their role as a team member and who are skilled in the art of negotiation and working with other people in a cooperative manner are most likely to feel that their IEP or 504 meetings are successful.

As one administrator stated, "When you are not working as a partnership, you aren't going to be effective as a team!" Parents are certainly key players in this process because they have the most knowledge and understanding of their child. Many times, parents also have the most knowledge about their child's disability. Teachers have a key role in this process because they see and work with your child in a school environment for a major part of the day. They have knowledge and understanding about how children learn and effective ways to teach. Administrators have knowledge of resources that are available to the district and what dollar amounts can be committed to various programs.

Problems can happen when parents become emotionally involved; though often times, it is hard not to. Parents have a vested interest in the outcome of the meeting because it's their child. If you are to be respected as a team player, however, you need to participate in the meeting exactly as you would participate in a meeting at your place of work. Be professional: try not to lose your cool or become tearful. You have a right to expect that type of behavior from the school staff present at the meeting as well.

Example I:

Melissa, parent of a ten-year old boy listened patiently (and painfully) as the art teacher in her son's elementary school described at length how disrespectful her son had been a few days ago in class. She was invited to attend a meeting with the teacher and the principal to discuss the consequences her son would receive because of poor behavior. Melissa, however, heard a different version of the same incident from at least three other children-all of whom had substantiated her son's version of the story. Melissa knew that the teacher was exaggerating and was not being entirely truthful with some of the particulars of the incident, but she kept her cool and let her continue with her story. When the teacher had finished, Melissa began to ask poignant questions about some of her statements, pointing out some inconsistencies. The teacher became agitated, rolled her eyes and began acting as if she was insulted by her questions. Melissa calmly said, "Mrs. Reed, I listened to your version of the story, and I have some questions for you. I expect you to be professional and answer them respectfully as I have provided you with the same courtesy for the last twenty minutes." If Melissa had screamed that the teacher was lying and that the other students had told her exactly what really happened, she would not have been as effective. At the conclusion of the meeting, the principal agreed to release the student from any consequences for his behavior.

Difficulties also happen when some team members assume roles that make other team members feel infringed upon or defensive.

Mary and her husband Joe have a five-year old child with autism who is entering kindergarten next school year. They have attended many seminars and training sessions and felt they had a good understanding of autism. Indeed, they are regarded as experts by many in this field. When they attended their child's transition meeting, Mary and Joe immediately assumed that the district did not know enough about the disorder, provided them with three video-tapes and several books and insisted that the team members use the materials to 'get trained.' What Mary and Joe did not realize was that last school year, the kindergarten teacher had had another child with autism in her classroom. This teacher had attended two trainings that Mary had also attended and was provided with consultative services throughout the school year from an autism specialist. Their overbearing approach turned the team off, just as it would in any team process. A better approach would be for Mary and Joe to have used the questioning technique to determine how much the staff knew about their son's disability:

Parent: "Have you ever worked with a child with autism?"

Teacher: "Why, yes! I actually had a student last year in my class with this disability."

Parent: "Was the child mild or severely autistic?"

Teacher: "He was mildly affected. His diagnosis was autism/Asperger's."

Parent: "My son is actually an autism/Asperger's child as well; however, he has a great deal of sensory processing issues that concern me."

Teacher: "What type?"

Parent: "He has a lot of trouble with loud, sudden noises and echoes. I think he is going to have a really hard time during a fire drill or if he were asked to sit through a noisy assembly. He may even have trouble in the gym or cafeteria. He will cover his ears, probably cry or maybe even get aggressive."

Teacher: "My previous student had some problems with smell, but not to the degree you are describing. Let me write that down, we will need to be aware of that and add some things into the IEP to help prepare us for that type of situation."

Parent:
"I have a small brochure that really describes my child's sensory problems (author's note: She didn't say 'children with autism'). I have attended several trainings and have implemented some of the suggestions at home, and they work for us! I highlighted which ones I thought you might like to try. Would you like to read it?

Teacher:
"Sure! Especially if it pertains to your child. I don't have the time during my work hours to read a lot of books and watch videos where I may only glean one or two things to help a student, and the majority of it is theory or doesn't apply to him/her. Thanks! This really helps!"

Guiding Star #2:
Come prepared to your meeting with your goals: Give preparation for the meeting priority status!

Example III:

Ryan's parents were very concerned about his grades. They made an appointment to meet with the school staff at 8:00 a.m. They were fifteen minutes late arriving to school, forgot to bring samples of the work that concerned them and then stopped and chatted with another child's parents in the school entrance way for a lengthy time. The principal was frustrated because the teachers had to return to their classrooms at 8:30, and the classroom teacher was perturbed because she had preparations to do before the children arrived. The parents left the meeting feeling as if it was rushed and nonproductive.

It is a given that most meetings will be held before or after school. These times are the times when most school staff are available to meet. Parents need to plan for babysitters and other "emergencies" so that the meeting is given priority treatment. If your meeting is at 8:00 a.m., that means the meeting starts at 8:00 a.m., not 8:10 or 8:15. By the same token, families have a right to expect the same treatment, especially if they are losing work time or being inconvenienced to meet at certain times of the day to accommodate staff. Although the meeting should be held at a mutually agreed upon time, usually one party will have to be more accommodating. If you are continually meeting at times that accommodate only school staff, you have a right to ask them to accommodate you as well. Cancellations on either side should be few and far between. Once you have committed to the date and time, keep it.

Make the most of your meeting. Bring pertinent documents or examples of your child's work that concerns you. Do not digress from the topic at hand and avoid lengthy chit-chat. If you feel that too much of the meeting is ending up this way, say, "It's great that Johnny is doing so well with his grades, but I feel that I still have not obtained an answer to my question about how we can improve his social skills. I don't want to go away and then have to call you to re-convene because I know you are busy and so am I." Parents can often set the tone for the meeting by stating why they called the meeting and what they hope to accomplish. In other words: State your goal for the meeting.

Julia was a very organized parent. When she asked to meet school staff, she would often type a small agenda and pass one out to each staff member. (Note: Julia's agenda rarely contained more than five points.) She would begin by referring staff to her concerns on the agenda and would gently urge them to keep to the topic of discussion. (Ex.: "Yes, that's mentioned in Point #4, but can we finish Point #2 first?") If her concerns were not all addressed by the end of the designated period, she would ask for another meeting to resolve the remaining issues. At first, this really surprised school personnel. Later, however, they came to respect Julia's "straight to the point" attitude and worked with her to see that her agenda was completed.

Example V:

At the conclusion of every meeting, Michael, a parent of a third-grade child with Asperger's, would summarize the results of the meeting: "O.K., you have agreed to give Joshua some more support in the recess setting by engaging some peers to work with him, and I have

agreed to make up that checklist that we would like to see completed

by the recess attendant to monitor his interactive skills over the next

few weeks. Is that correct?" Michael would then follow up in letter

form with the summarization and complete his part of the agreement

as soon as possible.

Guiding Star #3:
Make sure you are dealing with the right person in the special education chain.

Often times parents do not understand the chain of command in their school

district. When problems surface, they feel that the person they should call is the

director of special education, not realizing that a certain protocol needs to be

followed, just as it would in an office. If you are having a problem with your

child's teacher or something that's going on in the classroom, the first thing you

need to do is schedule a meeting with that teacher. If that meeting is not

productive or you feel that you are still having difficulty, schedule a meeting with

the teacher and the principal. If after that meeting you feel that you are no

closer to resolution of the problem, speak with the director of elementary education (or secondary education if that be the case), but be sure to explain that you have had meetings with both the teacher and the principal. Then, if you still feel that you aren't getting anywhere, the director of special education would be the next stop. Parents often express to the author that their meetings are "loaded up with people," and they feel intimidated and threatened. Upon further questioning, there are often reasons why this happens: parents have called four or five different individuals and suddenly a small incident turns into a full-blown problem.

Example VI:

Sheryl was having difficulty with her daughter Abby's Spanish teacher. Sarah was frustrated with the work and would often cry and become emotional in class. After the third such incident, Sheryl had enough. She contacted the principal in anger and demanded to know why the Spanish teacher was picking on Abby. The principal explained that she would speak with the Spanish teacher and call Sheryl back. A few days later, the principal called Sheryl to discuss the problem, and Sheryl felt that she was taking the teacher's side, and Sheryl became angry. She then contacted the director of special education for the district, who, after hearing Sheryl's concerns, asked the principal to schedule a meeting with the parents. When Sheryl came to the meeting (her husband was unable to attend), she felt completely intimidated because the teacher, the principal and the director of special education were all present.

Example VII:

Wendy called the office of the school's elementary school to schedule a time when she could come in and observe the kindergarten classroom. Her child with special needs would be enrolled there in the fall, and she wanted to get a good idea as to how the program operated. She had a lengthy discussion with the school secretary about her child's special needs and what she felt he would need in the classroom. The school secretary informed Wendy that she didn't know if the school would be able to provide all of the services Wendy wanted for her child. Wendy did not understand that the school secretary had no say in the delivery of special education services and that these decisions were made through an IEP team process. Wendy called the director of special education and informed him that she would not tolerate discrimination of her child because of his disability. Already, the team process was compromised.

No one likes to have their toes stepped on or feel as if they are out of the loop when it concerns something that pertains to them. Be sure that you respect the individual's feelings by dealing with him/her directly before moving up the ladder to the next level.

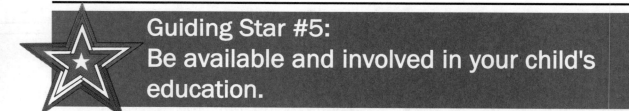

Guiding Star #5:
Be available and involved in your child's education.

It has been documented over and over that the children whose parents are most involved with their education are the children who will be most successful in the school setting. The author has heard some parents comment that he/she is not a teacher: 'It's the teacher's job to teach, not mine.' Some take an inactive role in monitoring study skills and homework, do not participate in any school activities (PTA or PTO functions), do not keep a close eye on the child's progress or provide any type of educational stimulation outside the school environment. When their child is absent, they do not concern themselves with what work was missed. Children with special needs need all of the above. Unfortunately, if these children are to progress, they need more support and assistance than typical children do. That assistance and support has to come from the home environment too. If your child's teacher makes an effort to contact you or wants to meet with you, by all means schedule a meeting! That teacher cares about your child, or she wouldn't be going the extra mile.

Example VIII:

Pamela was a single mom of a child with autism. She worked full time in a busy office. School staff asked if Pamela could be available every other week to discuss her daughter's progress. Pamela explained to them that she could not afford to miss work but offered to call in on her lunch hour. This was time-consuming for Pamela, but she felt that it was very important to demonstrate to the school that her daughter's educational progress was a priority to her. School staff agreed to be available at this time, put Pamela's call on speaker phone and held

the meeting in this manner so they could obtain her input.

What Pamela demonstrated to her school district was that she was serious

about her daughter's education and that she was willing to continue in a team

fashion to ensure her progress.

Guiding Star #6:
Dot your "I's" and cross your "T's."

As stated in Chapter Three, document, document, document. Do not mail

any copies of letters or evaluations to your district unless you keep a copy for

yourself. If you have phone conversations with teachers or administrators, always

reiterate those conversations back in letter form so that there is a record of the

conversation.

April 3, 2003

Mrs. Rudolph
Robertson Elementary School
300 School Road
Smithville, FL 15066

Dear Mrs. Rudolph:

Thank you for calling to speak with me concerning our son's behaviors. I was disappointed to learn that he is acting out so aggressively with his peers and discussed it with him last night. This is the third time you have had to call this month, and we are getting concerned.

Larry seems to be extremely frustrated with math. If you notice, he often tends to get aggressive during this time of the day. As I mentioned to you on the phone, my husband and I agree that he needs some additional supports for this class. You mentioned that perhaps Larry could attend the learning support classroom during this time.

We also feel that since Larry's behaviors are escalating, we need to develop a behavior support plan for him. Although we don't condone his behaviors, we feel that there is a reason why he is becoming more aggressive, and we need to be conscious of that as a team.

Please call at your earliest convenience to schedule an IEP meeting. We will be looking forward to hearing from you soon.

Sincerely yours,
Cynthia Vincent

Figure 4.1

Keep a small notebook by the phone to jot down pertinent points of conversations. Make sure you make a note of the date the phone call took place. You may need records of these conversations when you asked for additional services for your child.

Example IX:

Ashley was concerned about her daughter's social skills development. Apparently, so was Ashley's teacher. Ashley had had several phone conversations with her concerning her daughter's social problems at recess and lunch period. When the IEP meeting took place, Ashley called upon the teacher to help support her wish for a behavioral support plan for her daughter. The teacher did not recall many of the phone conversations that Ashley indicated pointed the need for such a plan. Ashley felt betrayed and frustrated when the team did not agree to provide her daughter with the added supports.

The extra time that you devote to documenting and detailing pertinent information will be well worth the effort.

Guiding Star #7:
Educate yourself so you can educate others.

It is so important that you know how to come to the table and discuss how

your child's disability will manifest itself in the classroom. Giving teachers a book

to read, a video to watch, or a packet to read about your child's disability, for

instance, will mean very little to him or her. Each child is an individual. As an

example, children who have diabetes are very different from one another. So are

children with autism spectrum disorders. What teachers need to understand is

how the child's disability is going to impact on them in the classroom. Educate

yourself on how your child's deficits will need to be addressed in their classroom.

Consider the following excerpts from a parent's IEP conference conversations:

Mrs. Reed (teacher): "I watched a video-tape this summer about

autism/Asperger's syndrome. It was really

fascinating but a lot to digest. In my classroom,

we do a lot of group and hands-on activities.

I'm worried that it will be too noisy for him."

Nichole (mom):   "Actually, Todd loves hands-on things. He is very well-behaved and does not have a lot of sensory challenges. His deficits involve social skills."

Mrs. Reed (worried):   "Oh . . . do you mean he's aggressive?"

Nichole: "Oh no! He will appear to you to be a very quiet child. He prefers to be on his own. He doesn't really know how to interact with other children on their terms. He can carry on a good conversation about computers, but beyond that, he's lost. In fact, that's one of my goals for him this year is to help him develop more age-appropriate pragmatic skills. He's also very literal. He will do EXACTLY what you tell him to do and expect others to do it too."

Mrs. Reed (laughing):   "Well, I might enjoy having a student do that for a change."

Nichole (laughing):   "I see what you mean. But, seriously, what I was referring to is he might be the "rule policeman" in your class. He may get a little anxious if you have class rules and then allow the children to break them or ignore them. He will listen to what you say and live by every word. If you say that the class is going to recess at 12:10, then at 12:10 he will be expecting that and may become upset if it isn't just that way. He is very concrete; very black and white; no gray areas here! Also, any visual tools you use in your instruction will be of great help to him because he is so concrete."

Mrs. Reed: "I guess I will have to 'mean what I say and say what I mean?'"

Nichole: "Yes. Better still, 'show what I say and show

what I mean.' However, he is also going to have

to learn that there are exceptions to things. No

one can go through life expecting that

everything has to go a certain way."

It is also important that parents become educated in special education law.

Many states have advocacy organizations that will provide easy-to-read literature

free of charge. Be sure to attend trainings in your area to learn more. Meet with

other parents, learn from them; glean what you need to know from their

experiences. Immerse yourself in understanding special education procedures.

Don't rely on other people to help you through it. Advocates are great sources of

information, but too many parents depend on them to do the work for them.

Advocates aren't available every single time you need them or to attend every

meeting you will ever have during your child's school years. When you are

educated, you know what your child is entitled to.

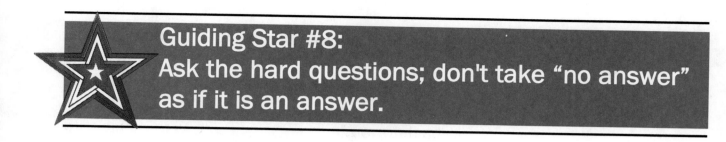

Guiding Star #8:
Ask the hard questions; don't take "no answer" as if it is an answer.

If you don't confront the problem, it never will get solved. Sometimes, parents have to be persistent to get things accomplished:

Sally (parent):   "Mr. Richter, I'm calling because I see that my son's teachers have not been in-serviced on the behavior support plan as of yet."

Mr. Richter (principal):   "What makes you think that?"

Sally: "Because I asked Mrs. Smith, and she said she knows nothing about it. She had a problem in her classroom last week and didn't follow the protocol we had set up in the IEP meeting two weeks ago."

Mr. Richter:	"I'll speak with Mr. Rearick (the learning support teacher) and see why it wasn't arranged and get back to you."
Sally:	"What time will you be calling me?"
Mr. Richter:	"Oh, not today, probably tomorrow."
Sally:	"I don't want to miss your call, Mr. Richter, and I'm extremely busy the next few days. Can we set a phone appointment now? If you can't find out the information you need by then, just call me at the appointment time and tell me so."
Mr. Richter:	"O.K. How does 2:00 tomorrow sound?"
Sally:	"Perfect. I'll talk to you then."

Or, consider this mom's IEP meeting conversation:

Mom: "So, let me reiterate . . . you have agreed to purchase the visual motor software for the computer in Mrs. Dean's classroom, is that right?"

Principal: "Yes."

Mom: "When will you be ordering that software?"

Principal: "As soon as I have a purchase order."

Mom: "How long does that take?"

Principal: "Usually about two weeks."

Mom: "So the software will be here in two weeks?"

Principal: "No, that's just to have the purchase order made up. Then we have to mail the purchase order into the company, and they have to ship the software. It could be several weeks once they get the purchase order before they ship it to us. Then we have to arrange for the software to be installed."

Mom: "Could we fax it to them instead? Can you call the company's 800 number here on the brochure and ask them how long it takes to ship? Then, perhaps we can get a rough idea when it will be here and have the computer support individual lined up to install it. I know from past experience, you have to be on his schedule to arrange for an installation."

Principal: "I don't know what the district's policy is with regards to faxing invoices."

Mom: "Do you want me to call your finance department and ask them since I have the catalog here?"

Principal: "No. I will take care of that. Give me the catalog."

Mom: "Great! Thank you! Is it O.K. if I call you on Wednesday to see how we're doing with that?"

Principal: "I guess so."

Parents should also be careful to ask one question at a time and wait for an answer before asking another:

Mom: "Mrs. Smith, does my child ever appear to be inattentive; does he fidget too much in your class?"

Mrs. Smith: "No."

Mom: "So you are saying that he's just about the

                    same as most children in your classroom?"

Mrs. Smith: "Yes."

See how much better this line of questioning would be if it went this way:

Mom: "Mrs. Smith, I noticed last week when I was

                    helping in your classroom that Michael seems

                    to be inattentive at times. Do you see this too?"

Mrs. Smith: "Yes, I do."

Mom: "Does he fidget excessively?"

Mrs. Smith: "No, I think all second graders are fidgety!"

Mom: "But when I saw him, I took a look around and thought he was more fidgety than most of the boys in his class, what do you think?"

Mrs. Smith: "Well, at times, yes, he his. But, you have to look at the big picture. His grades are very good. His social skills are coming along."

Mom: "Yes, but if we can improve his attention span, and he can become better at self-regulation, don't you think we should try to do this? He's only in second grade; the work is going to get tougher."

Mrs. Smith: "What did you have in mind?"

Parents can also remember that there will be times when school staff may not be as direct as they would like when answering their questions. You will need to be prepared for this and should insist politely that your questions be answered.

Cynthia: "Mrs. Dunmire, I am wondering if the social skills program we designed has been implemented as of yet."

Mrs. Dunmire: "Johnny is really improving in that area."

Cynthia: "Yes, but have the materials we ordered arrived yet?"

Mrs. Dunmire: "We have been devoting some attention this past month to eye contact and greeting peers."

Cynthia: "I'm sorry, but I feel that I have not gotten an

answer to my question, or it may be that I'm not

understanding your answer. Have we started

the pull out social skills class with peer

groups?"

Mrs. Dunmire: "Not yet."

The important thing to remember is that persistence is different from

abrasiveness. Again, treat the meeting as if it is a business transaction. In your

meetings with the school district, you have a right to know exactly what your child

is getting, how he will get it, when it is expected to be delivered and by whom.

Guiding Star #9:
Listen to team members!

If you have ever attended an IEP meeting, you will notice that very often

there are "camps." The administrators sit at one end of the table, the parents

and their advocate at another, the teachers and therapists at another. Often, this does not make for good communication or for open discussion. Although each

person sitting at the table is a team member, it often appears more like a

sporting event: the players of the team square off and face their adversaries on

the other side.

If you want to promote teamwork, accept the ideas and reasoning of the

other side. Listen, first. Formulate your response after you have heard and

digested what they have to say. If you are not ready to answer, say that you

would like a little bit of time to go home and think about what they are saying and

ask to meet again. This will give the appearance that you have weighed their

responses and have given careful consideration to the plan they propose. There

is nothing wrong with this.

Principal: "Mr. Aiken, the team truly feels that it would be

best for your son if he was placed in the autistic

support classroom."

Mr. Aiken:	"Well, I'd like to remind you that I am a part of the team too, but I will give careful consideration to your thoughts. Why do you feel this way?"
Principal:	"I'm sorry, you are right. You are a team member; I meant the school staff. We feel that Randy could benefit from the extra support we could provide him there behaviorally and academically."
Mr. Aiken:	"Specifically what supports?"
Principal:	"If Randy were to be placed in this classroom, he would have more structure. His teacher would be trained in working with children like Randy. There are fewer children there, and he would get more individual attention."

Mr. Aiken: "I can understand the smaller student/teacher ratio, but I don't understand the training part. Don't school personnel who feel that they need more support to work with a special needs child have the right to ask that they be provided with this training?"

Principal: "Well, yes, they do, but Randy's needs are great."

Mr. Aiken   "You mentioned behavioral supports. Randy doesn't even have a behavior plan now! How do we know that if we develop one and get an expert in here to help us that he won't need to change placement?"

Principal: "Well, we don't, but all that takes time, and Randy's behaviors are really becoming a problem."

Mr. Aiken:	"I guess we should have met earlier when this wasn't so critical. Why didn't you call me to schedule a meeting?"
Principal:	"We wanted to do everything we could do as a team before we called you."
Mr. Aiken:	"You keep saying 'team.' I'm a little bit upset that you didn't think we as his parents might have something to offer that might help you. What exactly have you tried?"
Principal:	"Well, we did try time-outs, but they aren't effective. We tried a token system where Randy could earn stickers for good behavior."

Mr. Aiken:	"This is what I meant. Did you know that Randy hates stickers? The glue residue really bothers him. Further, I guess what I meant was what strategies have you put in place so he doesn't misbehave? Time-outs are consequences. Why do you think he is misbehaving in the first place?"
Principal:	"We think the work is too hard."
Mr. Aiken:	"Now I'm really confused. His grades are "B's" and "C's" He's not failing anything."
Mr. Aiken:	"Since my wife is not here today, I would really like to go home and talk this over with her and then meet again with you later on in the week. I'd also like to be able to go and observe this proposed placement. Is that possible?"

Principal: "I can understand that. I will call you on

Wednesday to set up a new meeting date and a

time when you can go and observe the

classroom."

Mr. Aiken: "Thank you. I'll be looking forward to that call."

Mr. Aiken can then go home and think about the school's rationale away

from the charged moment of the meeting. He does not have to make a decision

at this point. He has made some valid points as a team member. More

importantly, he has really listened to the district's side. He can decide what his

answers will be based on the information that was presented to him. For the

reader's information, Mr. and Mrs. Aiken thought about the new placement. They

visited the setting. They felt that it was too restrictive for their son. They asked

for a functional behavior assessment, the development of a behavioral support

plan for their child and argued that the district needed to bring in an autism

consultant to help maintain Randy's placement in the least restrictive

environment before considering an alternative placement. Today, although Randy still has occasional behavioral challenges, his teacher feels that she is able to achieve meaningful progress for him in his regular education classroom.

Parents who visit proposed classrooms are not committing to them-in fact, as one advocate put it, you have to know what to say "no" to and why!

Guiding Star # 10:
Give credit where credit is due.

There will always be those individuals who go the extra mile for your child. Be sure that you single them out for the "above and beyond" work that they have done for your son or daughter. Write a letter of praise to his/her supervisor. In this way, you are differentiating them from team members who are doing the bare minimum of their job without laying blame. Individuals who are dedicated and devoted often experience burnout and need a pat on the back to let them know that they are truly effective in the lives of children like yours. Notes to their supervisors show that you recognize what they have done and value it. At the same time, they subtly convey to the other team members that you notice who is going the extra mile for your child! Be genuine with your praise. Being overly flattering may compromise extra supports you are trying to achieve for your son or daughter. Consider the family, for example, who wrote a glowing letter to their child's teacher, thanking her for all she had done for their child. Later, in a due process hearing, they tried to show that the supports the school had provided were not enough. Sometimes, telling the teacher personally how you feel might be a better solution.

In conclusion, it is critical that parents develop their own style of advocacy as a team player for their son or daughter. If the above suggestions make you uncomfortable for one reason or another, adapt them or change them. When you participate in a school meeting for your child, you should feel as confident as possible. School staff will need to learn how to adapt their own meeting style to you as well so that the team process can be effective. If you continually feel threatened or that your opinions/suggestions are not being considered, you may need to ask the district to bring in a mediator or someone who is trained in conflict resolution. Such an individual will know how to seek out middle ground when tensions rise high. Many communities also have educational advocates available to attend meetings with parents.

Chapter Five

Developing the IEP

Goals and Objectives

Specially Designed

Instruction

The individualized education plan (IEP) is the roadmap for your child's education. It charts a path through the classroom curriculum, sets goals at your child's ability level and determines how the curriculum will be modified and adapted for your child's unique learning needs. The "meat and potatoes" of the IEP are the goals and objectives. Goals that are written vaguely and are nonspecific make it difficult to measure the student's progress. Goals that are written in measurable terms describe specifically what the student is expected to do and how well. The "Present Levels of Performance" section of the IEP details at what level the student is currently performing in key areas of their disability (reading, math, social skills). Annual goals should take the student from this present level of performance and detail what we want the student to accomplish in a nine-month period.

The short-term objectives or benchmarks of an IEP serve as a compass for reaching the annual goals and also serve as a means to measure progress towards those goals. Parents should understand that if their child does not meet the annual goals or short-term objectives within the school year, it does not mean that the school district is liable for not providing an appropriate education. It may mean that the team overestimated the student's abilities, especially if he did make progress towards those goals. It may also mean that the student learns material slower than the team expected. If that is the case, the IEP team should re-open the document and revise the goals and objectives. If year after year, however, the student does not make progress towards their goals and objectives, it might be that their placement or program is not appropriate. At this point, it might also be assumed that the school district is liable for not having developed an appropriate program in which the student could make progress.

Parents often ask if the goals and objectives should be based on the regular education curriculum or if they should be based on the student's current ability level. The answer is the student's current level of performance. If, for instance, the IEP states that Johnny is reading on a beginning first-grade level but is placed in the second-grade curriculum, we can be sure that it will be extremely difficult for Johnny to meet his goals and objectives. The curriculum has to match Johnny's ability level, not the other way around. Students with disabilities need to have materials and instruction provided at their current level of performance. In many IEP's, the "Present Levels of Performance" is not written specifically. Parents have no way of knowing, year after year, if their child's academic skills are improving. They may be meeting their annual goals and objectives, but they still may not be keeping up with their same-age peers.

The author once sat in on an IEP meeting where the parent of a seventh grader expressed concern that her son's goals and objectives were so easily obtainable and so vaguely written year after year. He was receiving modified grades and frequently achieved "A"'s and "B"'s in reading on his report card. When the parent asked about her son's "Present Level of Performance," she was shocked to learn that he was only reading on an end of second-grade level and had really not improved from that level in five years! The author helped her to write goals based on the third-grade curriculum so that she could see at the end of the school year if her son had progressed to this end of third-grade level of performance.

Here is an example of a poorly-written "Present Level of Performance" section of the IEP:

"Johnny is currently making an "A" in reading, a "B" in science and a "B" in math in his learning support classroom. He completes all assignments and participates well in class."

What we have learned from the above is that Johnny is performing well in his learning support classroom, but is he learning the same material as his same-age peers? What grade-level materials is Johnny using in his learning support classroom?

Now, here is an example of a better-worded "Present Level of Performance" section of the IEP:

"Johnny is currently make an "A" in reading and is performing at a second grade, fourth-month level in reading fluency. His reading comprehension is also at a second grade, fourth-month level. He is making a "B" in math and is performing at a second grade, first month-level in this subject. Johnny completes all assignments and participates well in class." (Note: Johnny is in third-grade, first month. What we have learned in this example is that Johnny is not learning at

90

the same rate as his typical peers. His grades have been modified to reflect his learning level. Now, we need to determine what specific math skills Johnny has mastered and what skills he still has difficulty with.)

Using the above information obtained from the better-worded "Present Level of Performance," here is an example of a good annual goal and some measurable short-term objectives for Johnny's reading comprehension:

Annual Goal:

Johnny will improve his reading comprehension from a second grade, fourth-month level to a third grade, first-month level. (Johnny should be able to expect nine months' growth in a program that is suited to his needs.)

1. Johnny, using a story map, will be able to identify the characters of a story and describe two personality traits each, four out of five times weekly.

2. Johnny will be able to underline the main idea of a story or paragraph, four out of five times weekly.

3. Given a short story, Johnny will be able to predict the outcome or offer a plausible ending to this story, four out of five times weekly.

4. After reading a short story, Johnny will be able to sequence the order of events, out of five times weekly.

(Note: These were the tasks that a third-grade student should be able to do if he is successful in reading comprehension. This information was gleaned from the reading curriculum booklet provided by Johnny's school district. If Johnny is not able to do one of the above, then these skills can be individually targeted for extra support.)

For emphasis, the following is an example of a poorly written annual goal and short-term objectives for the above present level of performance.

Annual Goal:

Johnny will improve his reading skills to a third-grade level. (Notice that this could mean a beginning third-grade level or an end of third-grade level).

1.   Johnny will be able to read a short passage and answer comprehension questions, four out of five times weekly. (Note: Does this mean that Johnny will correctly answer these comprehension questions four out of five times weekly or that he will just answer them? What if Johnny can't answer the questions? What skills is he missing? Would this be better as an annual goal? Isn't fluency different from comprehension?)

2.   Johnny will be able to identify letter sounds, four out of five times weekly. (Note: What letter sounds? What if he is better at identifying vowel sounds vs. blends? Again, what if he identifies them wrong? Is he meeting the goal then?)

3. Johnny will be able to read third-grade sight words 100% of the time. (Note: remember, though, that Johnny is only at a second grade, fourth-month level. Also, this objective, again, does not reflect at what expected level of achievement Johnny will be expected to perform.)

4. Johnny will participate in the "Drop Everything and Read" program weekly. (Note: What does participate mean? If he chooses a book to read and reads one page he's met the goal!)

Generally, parents are not experts in knowledge of school curriculum and may certainly feel at a disadvantage when goals and objectives are being written. It is often helpful to pose questions to teaching staff when writing the IEP goals. For instance, "What specific things does one need to be able to do in third grade to be successful at reading?" Very often teachers may respond in this manner: 'Children need to be able to read 300 sight words' or 'Children need to be able to find the main idea of a paragraph.' These responses can be used to write the goals. This is one reason why it is extremely important that regular education teachers be present at IEP meetings.

Schools usually have curriculum guidelines that are available for parents to review. Very often teaching objectives are included in these curriculum guidelines and provide a useful framework in developing goals.

Expected Levels of Achievement/Performance

Short-term objectives and benchmarks must be accompanied by an expected level of achievement. The expected level of achievement can be a percentage that the child is expected to reach or a numerical value (four out of five times daily, weekly or monthly, etc.) The expected level of achievement needs to "make sense" in terms of the objective:

The following is an example of a poorly worded short-term objective and expected level of achievement:

Short-term Objective:

"Joshua will improve knowledge of letter sound relationships.

Expected Level of Achievement: 83%."

(Note: The Expected Level of Achievement chosen is very confusing here. What level is he currently working from, and how was 83% chosen? Does it mean that he will improve 83% from his baseline level, or does this mean that given letter sounds, Joshua will be able to read them with 83% accuracy?)

The following is an example of a good short-term objective and expected level of achievement:

Short-term Objective:

"Given a random list of ten fourth-grade words previously presented, Matthew will be able to correctly read them within fifteen seconds.

Expected Level of Achievement: 90%."

(Note: Matthew will be able to read nine out of ten words in fifteen

seconds.)

Method of Evaluation

The IEP team should also decide how the objectives will be measured. Every

short-term objective will need to have a way that it can be measured. If the team

is having trouble deciding how to measure the objective, it might be that the

objective is not written in a measurable manner:

Here is an example of a poorly worded short-term objective and its method

of evaluation:

Short-term Objective:

"Sean will improve his social skills. Expected Level of Achievement:

90%. Method of Evaluation: observation."

(Note: This is a huge target area: All of Sean's social skills will improve 90%! However, at what level is he functioning now? Specifically, how is the staff going to determine that he has improved 90% from this level?)

Here is a better example:

Short-term Objective:

"Sean will greet a peer daily at recess, or when he arrives at school. Expected Level of Achievement: four out of five times weekly. Method of Evaluation: teacher observation/charting."

(Note: Now we know that the target social goal is for Sean to greet peers when he comes to school and at recess. His teacher will chart his progress daily.)

Here are some examples of specific ways that progress can be evaluated and measured:

- Teacher observation.

- Student self-monitoring sheet.

- Teacher-made tests.

- Chapter tests/quizzes.

- Teacher probes. (Note: When the teacher calls on or "probes" the student for a response.)

- Checklists.

- Rubrics. (Note: Rubrics are a list of requirements as to how students will earn their grades. For instance, for an "A" grade in an assignment that involved writing a report, the rubrics might be: the report should be typed, should be at least six paragraphs long with each paragraph containing at least four sentences and have a bibliography page that contains three references.)

How Progress Will be Reported

Many IEP's call for progress reporting to occur at the end of the marking period through report cards (either every six or nine weeks). Parents do have the option, however, to ask for more frequent progress reporting either through anecdotal notes sent home via the student's book bag or through the mail, phone calls, e-mails, checklists of goals or any other means the IEP team decides. This method of progress reporting should be in addition to the regular report card progress reporting. Parents of children with disabilities are entitled to receive progress on their child's goals and objectives, not just their report card grades.

Progress is to be reported at least as often as parents of typical students receive progress.

Some parents devise their own methods of progress reporting. For instance, one parent wanted to know specifically how her child was doing at recess with regard to social goals. She did not want to wait every nine weeks to see if her son was improving in this area. At the same time, the IEP called for a method of evaluation of teacher observation. By using a checklist, the teacher would observe the child to see if he was mastering the targeted goals, and then report his progress to the parent via a copy of the checklist weekly. The parent proposed the use of the checklist system and actually designed it for them. All the staff then had to do was copy and use it daily to record progress:

DAILY SOCIAL SKILLS CHECKLIST					
	MON	TUE	WED	THU	FRI
Greeted a peer upon arrival					
Offered a compliment					
Joined in play when invited					
Initiated a Conversation					
Refrained from interrupting					
Teachers Comments					

Figure 5.1

Program Modifications and Specially Designed Instruction

Special education services must be provided free of charge to parents. Program modifications are to be provided to meet the individual needs of children with disabilities. For instance, a child with ADHD (attention deficit hyperactivity disorder) might require preferential seating close to the teacher or worksheets free of visual clutter. A child with autism might require oral directions accompanied by written directions. Or, they might require a picture schedule of their day to assist them in periods of transition. Specially designed instruction also should include ways that the curriculum will be adapted to suit the needs of a child with a disability to enable them to achieve in the general education environment.

The contents of the ER report usually detail the child's need for program modifications. Often specific recommendations are included in the report for this section of the IEP. If a child, for instance, is diagnosed with both autism/Asperger's syndrome and attention deficit, he is entitled to accommodations for both types of disabilities in their IEP. However, the district only needs to provide these accommodations if the ER report acknowledges two prongs: the presence of both disabilities and that they both require specially designed instruction. In some cases, the child may only qualify for an IEP to address one disability. The other disability may need to be addressed in a 504 Agreement. Earlier in the book, the author mentioned that the ER report is the blueprint for the services provided in the IEP. If the ER report does not contain such recommendations, you most likely are not going to be able to ask for them in the IEP.

Program modifications and specially designed instruction techniques should be written to include recommendations for the regular education classroom as well when the student is being included in these types of classroom. Children do not have their disabilities in only certain rooms of the school building. The general education curriculum also needs to be modified or adapted to accommodate deficit areas so that these children can be successful in these environments as well.

Chapter Six

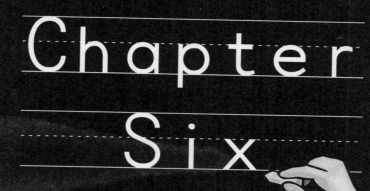

Supports for
Personnel
Supports for
Students

Parents as Educators

As was stated in previous chapters, you, as parents, are an integral component of the individualized education planning team that will help to shape the course of your child's educational program. Parents should never be underestimated for the wealth of information they can provide to school staff. They may not hold degrees in education, be knowledgeable about curriculum design and development or be behavioral specialists. But they are experts in knowledge of their child. They know their child's strengths, problem areas, learning style and what motivates them. If the team does not welcome parent input, they are missing out on an opportunity to be able to design the most effective program for students. Ensuring that parents are included in the team process as valuable members is not only the most appropriate way to go when designing special education programs for students with disabilities, it is a fundamental component of IDEA. School districts that do not accept the team process as their fundamental rule of thumb will soon discover that problems with trust will interfere fairly quickly with their ability to have productive meetings, establish realistic goals and maintain healthy communications between home and school.

Also included in previous chapters was advice on how parents should educate themselves so that they can educate others. It was emphasized that reading materials provided to school personnel should be concise; they should be pertinent and relative to their own child's manifestation of his/her disability. In other words, if you select a book for your child's teacher to read, the book should contain enough specific information that will be directly applicable to the job of teaching your child.

An important part of the individualized education plan (IEP) is often referred to as the "Supports for the Child Provided for School Personnel" section. This section is devoted to describing the ways that teachers and staff who work with the student will obtain the support that they need so that they are able to do their job effectively. It may include resource materials or equipment. It may also include in-service training, contracting the services of an outside consultant, attendance at conferences, or reading parent-provided literature, all of which is designed to help teachers and staff feel as if they have all the "tools" they need to work with your child.

Claire, a mother of a twelve-year old child with autism, makes a habit of requesting from her child's principal a half-hour school meeting at the start of the school year to speak with all of her child's teachers in one setting. Claire gives a brief talk about her son, includes a description of his diagnosis, a description of his interests and motivators, some predicted problem areas that the team may notice (for example, what happens if he experiences overload) and ways to address these concerns. She also explains how her son's social deficits may interfere with peer relationships and how staff can facilitate these interactions. Claire always asks one teacher from the last school year who was particularly effective with her son to take a few moments and share her thoughts as well with the new staff. Claire's teachers welcome her input. They feel it provides them with a brief "snapshot" of her child and some practical strategies that work with him. Often, the meetings run more than a half-hour because the staff is keenly interested/involved and want to learn more. This brief in-service also provides the added benefit of ensuring consistency *among staff as to how they will handle problem areas. It also helps to*

solidify the parent/staff collaborative relationship.

Parents can also gather together concise documentation of teaching techniques that are particularly useful their child. Because each child with autism/Asperger's is unique, ready-made curriculums are not as effective as educational programs designed specifically around the needs of each student.

Obtaining a small three-ring binder, limiting the material in scope and using bullets to describe strategies makes the information handy and easy to read.

This little reference manual can be organized in the following manner:

Page 1: Picture of the student, birth date, address, phone numbers, parent's names.

Page 2: Brief description of autism/Asperger's in teacher/friendly language.

Page 3: Strengths, motivators and the child's areas of interest.

Page 4: Areas of concern and suggestions that are effective in managing troublesome behaviors.

Page 5: Examples of teaching techniques/strategies that work well for your child.

Excerpts from these pages can also be used in the development of the IEP. For instance, items on Page 3 above can often be included in the section of the IEP that describes the child's strengths or the things that they do well. Items on Page 4 above can be used to develop a behavior support plan or to develop the section of the IEP that refers to how the child's disability affects progress in the classroom.

MY CHILD'S STRENGTHS AND INTERESTS

Many children with autism/Asperger's have special interests. These might be hobbies or things that the student likes to do or collect. These are often referred to as the child's "passions" because of the exceptional degree of interest and knowledge that the student has about them. Some of these interests may be unusual, and they are different from other children's interests. For example, one child with Asperger's we know collects sticks. In addition, some passions may not be age-appropriate; for example, a third-grade child who enjoys Sesame Street characters. In many cases, the "passion" can be a huge motivator to stay on task or participate in a nonpreferred activity. We can often get our son to clean up his room if he then earns a chance to do something with his passions.

My child has the following passions:

Enjoys anything having to do with the Civil War. (He has a vast store of knowledge about the war, and he can even tell you about each of the various battles!)

Has exceptional computer ability. (He began reading the DOS manual that came with our families' computer in kindergarten. He can troubleshoot many classroom computer problems.)

We encourage you to use our son's interests to further develop his social and academic skills, as they are strong motivators for him.

Figure 6.1

AREAS OF CONCERN

Our son has sensory issues, especially involving the sense of hearing and the sense of touch. In both areas, he is hypersensitive. Loud noises such as fire alarms, score boards in the gymnasium, band assemblies and shouting within confined areas will upset him. He may cover his ears, cry or scream because it hurts him. Please try to anticipate the above and excuse him from these types of activities.

His sense of touch is also pronounced. He will not enjoy pats on the back, even when you are congratulating him for doing a good job! He may swing out or try to hit people who touch him because he can't differentiate between this being deliberate or accidental: he does not enjoy this sensation! Please keep his seat away from main traffic areas in your room (such as where the garbage can or pencil sharpener are located) to risk having people "bump" him. Seat him next to kids who "stay within their space." Place him last in moving lines so there is less chance of him being bumped. We feel that occupational therapy may help him to be less overwhelmed with sensory issues.

Our son also has extreme difficulty being age-appropriate with social skills. He is just learning to speak with peers, but often does not greet them or follow through with conversations. He will need a social skills component to his IEP. He is also very literal: if you say we are moving to art at 10:00, he will be looking for that and expect it. He may get overwhelmed with too many changes to his day.

Figure 6.2

Parents can also go the extra mile by designing some visual supports (schedules, cue cards, etc.) or social stories or comic strips that may work for the child and provide these as examples on Page 5.

TEACHING TECHNIQUES THAT WORK WELL

Our son learns best when things are presented visually. He has difficulty attending to lengthy directions and will "shut down" when too much is presented to him in this manner. Providing him with directions both orally and in a written form (such as on the board, or on a piece of paper) will be helpful. If his desk is messy, providing him a visual map of what he needs the inside to look like (morning books on the left, afternoon books on the right) will help him keep it neater. Social skills, too, work better if they are presented visually. For instance, using cartoons or stick figures can be helpful:

No yelling or screaming in school!

Figure 6.3

Parents often complain that their input is not considered in the development of the IEP. If this information is provided to the team each year in the above manner, it can be readily incorporated into the document. All the parent needs to do is refer the team to their booklet.

Including Outside Resources

Today, many families utilize the supports offered by mental health professionals, behavioral specialists and therapeutic providers. These individuals, too, can serve as resources for teachers and other school staff on an as-needed basis or as a contract-related service provider. If the parents or other team members desire this input, their names or agency names can be included in this portion of the IEP. Many districts, however, will refuse to include these names in the document, as this may then be interpreted that they MUST use these particular resources. However, districts should rest assured that there are no duration and frequency time elements included in this section of the IEP. Neither does this section specify how these particular individuals will be consulted. So, if a school district lists that ABC agency is a support for school personnel, that simply means that ABC agency can be a consultant by phone, by letter or report, or be brought in and used "as needed" by school staff. If particular time elements have been agreed upon by the team and there is service to the student, this service then becomes a "Related Service" and should be written in the "Related Services" portion of the document. For instance, if a teacher needs the support of a behavior specialist, this is a "Support for Personnel." If, however, the behavior specialist is providing help to the student and faculty two times a week, this is a "Related Service."

Supports for Students

The "Related Services" portion of the IEP refers to any supportive service that is used to assist a student with a disability in the special education program and delivered in a specific manner and/or frequency. Such services may include some or all of the following:

- Special transportation to and from school.

- Speech/language services.

- Occupational therapy.

- Physical therapy.

- Social skills training.

- Job coaching.

- Vision services.

- Adaptive physical education.

- Parent counseling and training (which would include district-funded parent attendance at trainings or conferences).

- Social work services in school.

- Counseling.

Since these services are based on the individual needs of the student, this list is not definitive and can certainly include more items than those listed above. The IEP team decides which services the student needs in their educational environment. This portion of the IEP must list a location where each related service will be provided and the frequency for which they will be provided. A start and end date for each service must also be included if it is different from the start and ending date of the IEP.

Supports for personnel and related services for students with autism/Asperger's are often the glue that holds an individualized education plan together. Careful consideration needs to be given to these two very important sections of the student's IEP.

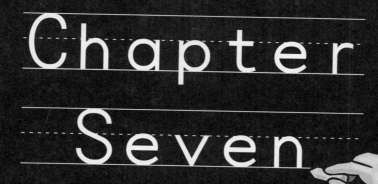

Chapter Seven

Designing a Social Skills Program

If your child has been diagnosed with an autism spectrum disorder or autism/Asperger's syndrome, they will need a social skills program in the school setting. This is one area that will need to be addressed early on. Parents need to understand that the child's deficits in this area will not automatically be remediated with maturity or by providing opportunities to interact with typical peers. [1]

Individuals with autism/Asperger's frequently show great deficits in their social skills even prior to entering school. For instance, a child at age one should be expected to regard faces as important, especially familiar ones. At age two, they should be expected to maintain attention to a speaker for 30+ seconds. At age five, they should be able to maintain active interest in a person for over a minute. Yet, these children often start school with very few of these expected skills. And too often, these skills are not even addressed as deficits in their educational programs.

---

[1] "Social Skills Training for Elementary School Autistic Children with Normal Peers," Social Behavior in Autism, Marian Wooten and Gary Mesibov, Plenum Publishing Corporation, 1986, p. 306.

Hilary was a five-year old child with Asperger's. She attended kindergarten at her local elementary school. Very early on, her teacher noticed that Hilary was not able to sit in circle time and participate in the morning routine. In circle time, she would participate in a five to ten-minute daily routine that included calendar and weather activities, a short song and current events (i.e. birthday recognitions and holiday discussions). Hilary would play with her shoes, hum to herself and appear detached from the group.

Social skill deficits will be blatantly apparent when children with autism/Asperger's begin to interact with typical kids. They may find it difficult to participate in imitative play (i.e. playing house or playing cowboys), or to take turns and/or play cooperatively. They may also find it difficult to follow through with or maintain certain play activities. As these children get older, there may be problems with reading social messages through body language and not knowing what is appropriate social behavior.

Michael, a nineteen-year old with Asperger's has learned that a good way to start a conversation with a woman is to ask her what her hobbies are. However, he frequently approaches strangers and asks them these questions.

As language develops (and sometimes it develops quite fluently), there will be problems with initiating and maintaining the topic of conversation, interpreting what is said literally, difficulty reading subtle messages (ex.: sarcasm), problems with recognizing facial expressions and voice inflections, perseveration on various topics and displaying unusual vocal qualities.

The author recommends that parents and teachers observe their child in unstructured (recess, play time) and structured (classroom) settings to discover three or four social skills deficits that can be addressed by school staff. Careful observation and "eavesdropping" on student conversations can give clues and help pinpoint troublesome areas to target for goals. Target skills should be age appropriate and directly related to the problem areas the child is experiencing at that time. Base line data should be collected so that progress can be measured.

Example III:

Lori observed Rose, her first-grade child, in the first part of her school day and at recess. She noticed that her daughter did not greet anyone when she entered the classroom. At recess, she did not initiate play with peers. If another child asked her daughter to join in, she would sometimes do so, but then she would wander off after a few minutes. The IEP team decided to address three goals for Rose: (1) Rose would be able to greet a peer and/or make a pleasant comment (2) Rose would be able to initiate play with a peer using an activity that she liked and (3) Rose would be able to maintain play with a peer for at least five minutes and end the play appropriately. Her IEP team provided individualized instruction on how to greet peers through a social story[2] and provided Rose with a list of pleasant comments. Rose role-played these greetings one-on-one with her classroom teacher. She also was scripted on ways to initiate and end play.

[2]Gray, Carol - "The New Social Story Book" Future Horizons, Inc., Publsiher 2002.

> *Although at first her actions seemed rather robotic, Rose eventually began to feel comfortable with her new-found skills and began to use them more naturally.*

Parents often express to the author that they are unsure about how to convince school staff to address social skills. The section in the IEP entitled "How the Student's Disability Affects Progress in the Classroom" is where the student's social deficits can be described and how these deficits will impact on the child's school day. Parents should remember that recess and lunch time are also important parts of the school day. By documenting how social skill deficits will impact on the student's functioning, the door can be opened for including social goals into the document.

In the book, Incorporating Social Goals in the Classroom-A Guide for Teachers and Parents of Children with High-Functioning autism/Asperger's Syndrome,[3] the author states that social skills are best taught when the skill is introduced in a one-on-one setting, practiced in a small group setting with typical children, then prompted and supported in the general education environment.

---

[3]Moyes, Rebecca, Incorporating Social Goals in the Classroom-A Guide for Teachers and Parents of Children with High-Functioning Autism/Asperger's Syndrome, Jessica Kingsley Publishers, 2001, p. 136.

Finding ways to discreetly cue the student in generalized settings will be necessary. Too often, teachers and parents resort to correcting or reprimanding the student verbally in such situations. This can be perceived as a punishment, when in fact, the student may not even realize what he is doing wrong. The methods of teaching social skills that work best are those that are visual and/or concrete. Consider the picture representation (figure 7.1) that was used for a child that had difficulty keeping to the topic of conversation:

The social goals need to be specific and address appropriately the child's developmental level in this area.

Example IV:

One child's IEP called for a goal that would address his ability to take on another child's perspective. In later years, this same goal appeared over and over in the child's IEP, and the team did not feel that he was making any progress in this area. Finally, an autism consultant pointed out to the team that being able to take on someone's perspective involves many types of mastered skills: being

When I talk with a friend, what I say is like throwing a ball in the air.

When my friend catches it, he will throw a "comment" or answer back. This is called having a conversation.

Then it will be my turn to catch the ball. If I don't answer or if I don't keep to the topic, I will be dropping the ball.

This will make my friend feel as if I don't want to talk to him any more. He may then go and talk to someone else.

I should always try to keep my conversation ball in the air!

Figure 7.1

able to read facial expressions, being able to read body language and being able to detect voice inflections as they pertain to emotions. The consultant pointed out that perhaps the student had not acquired those individual skills that would help him to be able to achieve mastery in perspective-taking. Although this child was now in the sixth grade, the team agreed that he was still unable to do many of the things listed above. The IEP was re-written to include better short-term objectives involving the missing skills, and soon the student began to make progress towards perspective taking.

The following is a list of social language deficits that could be addressed in an individualized education plan:

- Turn-taking in conversation.

- Preoccupation with certain topics of discussion.

- Literal understanding of language.

- Difficulty with prosody: the musical quality of the voice.

- Problems recognizing irony, figures of speech, sarcasm.

- Bluntness.

- Difficulty exhibiting joint attention.

Example V:

Jeffrey had a lot of trouble with being too literal. He would insist that the rules of the classroom be followed by every student and would frequently "tattle" on those who were not following the rules. If the teacher announced that the children would be going to art class in five minutes, he would be very upset if they did not move to the class at

> *that specific time. If his teacher told the class not to speak while waiting in line, he would not tell the cafeteria worker what he wanted for lunch because he was still waiting in line.*

In the example above, Jeffrey had to learn that there are exceptions to the rules and that sometimes things don't go as planned. Some of the things that the team felt might be useful were for Jeffrey to be provided with the class rule chart and to discuss with his teacher some of the rules that concerned him in order to get an idea of why he was being so literal. Jeffrey was quick to point out that the rule chart said 'no hitting/pushing' but he had previously witnessed this behavior on several occasions, and the children were not punished for breaking this rule. A photograph was taken of the playground monitor at recess and used to explain to Jeffrey in a visual manner how sometimes teachers can not possibly see every infraction of the rules on the playground because of her line of vision. Sometimes rules are broken. A Social Story™ [1] was written to describe who is in charge of the classroom and playground and what the teacher's role and the student's role is in both situations. A second story was developed to describe in detail when tattling is appropriate and when it isn't.

---

[1]Gray, C. New Social Stories - Illustrated - Future Horizons, Inc., Publisher 2002

A Social Story For Tattling

Tattling is when I tell the teacher or another grown up about something that someone is doing to get him to stop or to get him in trouble.

I may say, "Mrs. Smith, Johnny is spitting." Or, I might say, "Mrs. Smith, Rachel is chewing gum, and we aren't allowed to chew gum." These are two examples of tattling.

Most students do not like tattlers because usually tattling gets them in trouble. Then the students will probably be disciplined by the teacher.

If I tattle too much, it will be hard for me to get along with my friends.

There are several rules to think about before I tattle.

First, I should not tattle if the thing that the other student is doing is not causing me or anyone else harm. For instance, if a student is talking and the teacher said, "No talking." I should not tattle because the student is not causing me or anyone else harm. Even though the student is breaking a rule, it is not my job to stop him/her. I am not the boss.

I should tattle if someone is hurting me or damaging any of my things. For instance, if someone throws a stone at me, I should tell the teacher because throwing stones is dangerous. A stone could hurt me.

I should tattle if I see someone hurting someone else or damaging something that doesn't belong to them. For instance, if I see someone punching or hitting someone else, I should tell the teacher so she can stop this person from hurting the other person.

I know I can use these rules to help me decide if I should tattle.

Then, I can have fun with my friends!

Figure 7.2

133

Jeffrey also was encouraged to list other rules to add to the rule list so that he could begin to see that it is not possible to list every single rule on the rule chart. Jeffrey had to learn that rule charts are guidelines for good behavior: they are not all inclusive.

The team also decided it might be helpful for Jeffrey to begin to learn about idioms and figures of speech--what they mean and how they are applied. Jeffrey was also very literal with these as well. His team came up with a visual representation of several idioms. For instance, Jeffrey is 'down in the dumps.' What does 'down in the dumps' mean? Are you 'down in the dumps' when your parents take you to get an ice-cream cone? Are you 'down in the dumps' when you miss you favorite T.V. show? Does 'down in the dumps' mean that you are sad or at the place where they dump garbage?

The team came up with the annual goal of:

Annual Goal:

"Jeffrey will demonstrate a 50% improvement in his flexibility with classroom rules and routines from baseline data collected prior to instruction."

Short-term Objectives:

Jeffrey will be able to:

1. List five new rules that would be appropriate to add to the rule chart, three out of four times monthly.

2. List five exceptions to the rules on the rule chart, three out of four times monthly.

3. Describe correctly when it is appropriate to tattle and when it is not, three out of four times monthly.

4. Refrain from tattling at recess for inappropriate reasons, four out of five times weekly.

5. Identify the meaning of and use in conversation twelve popular idioms such as 'down in the dumps,' 'hang in there,' 'step on it,' three out of four times monthly.

Specially Designed Instruction/Program Modifications for Teaching Social Skills

The social stories and visual instruction tools used to teach social skills are listed in the "Specially Designed Instruction/Program Modifications" section of the IEP. This section of the IEP includes those methods of teaching that work for the child with autism/Asperger's and are unique to their way of learning. Specially designed instruction items include any type of modification to the curriculum that needs to be made to encourage a child to participate successfully in regular or special education classes and to assist them in meeting their goals.

Specially designed instruction items for social skills development could include:

- Individual and small group instruction.

- Visual representation of social skills through the use of social scripts, stories, comics and cue cards.

- Use of video-tape.

- Use of tape-recorders.

Some social behavior goals that could be addressed in the IEP include:

- Problems with perspective taking.

- Weakness in imitation and play skills.

- Demonstration of weak "affect" (the ability to use appropriate facial expressions).

- Inability to decipher the facial expressions and body language of others.

- Inability to read nonverbal gestures and cues.

- Difficulty practicing self-awareness.

- Difficulty controlling emotions.

- Poor eye gaze.

- Not recognizing when their behavior is socially inappropriate.

Example VI:

Luke was a child that had difficulty controlling his anxiety. When too many changes took place in his classroom or when things became too noisy, he would often react with a melt-down, falling to the floor, screaming or crying.

His IEP team decided that an annual goal would be included to help address Luke's inability to respond appropriately to stress. His short-term objectives included teaching Luke to recognize what signals his body gives when he is distressed, encouraging Luke to visually identify on a scale of one to ten where his stress lies, providing Luke with a list of strategies to put in place once he identified a certain stress level and helping Luke to recognize when he needed to go to a pre-arranged quiet spot. His specially designed instruction items included an identified quiet spot, a cue card of the quiet spot that Luke could present to the teacher when he was becoming anxious or the teacher could give to Luke when she felt he needed a break, a "stress meter" scale and a social story describing his body's stress signals.

What is My Stress Level Today?

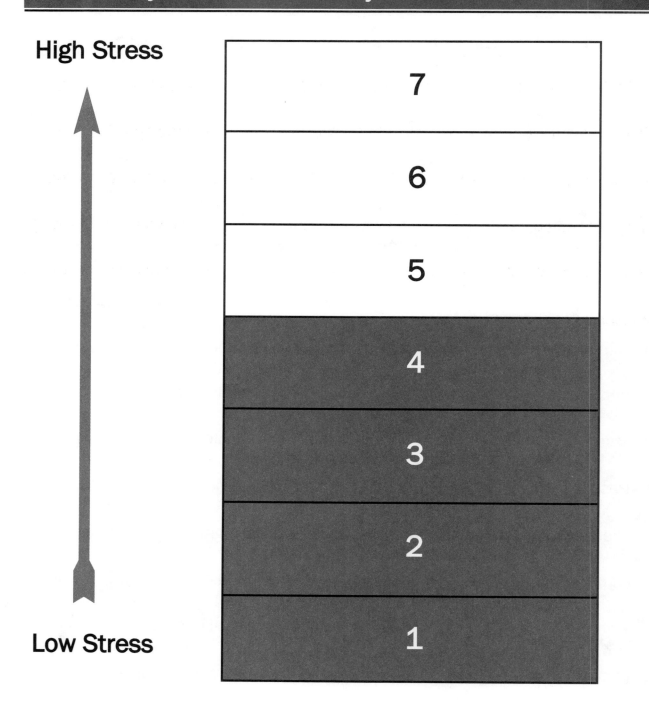

High Stress

| 7 |
| 6 |
| 5 |
| 4 |
| 3 |
| 2 |
| 1 |

Low Stress

Because Luke's inappropriate response to stress had been engrained for so long, it took several months for the team to notice progress in this area. Today, however, Luke can tell his teacher when he needs a break and identify on his scale how stressed he is.

Children with autism/Asperger's syndrome have social weaknesses. In fact, deficits in social language and social behavior are key diagnostic criteria for this disorder. School districts must make every attempt to evaluate all areas of the child's suspected disability and determine if deficits in social skills are impacting on the child's school day and if specially designed instruction or accommodations are required.

Chapter Eight

Teasing and Self Esteem

When typical children have lengthy interactions with children with high-functioning autism or autism/Asperger's syndrome, they often begin to notice their differences fairly quickly. In the later elementary and middle school years, social interactions with peers can often become problematic. Perhaps their idiosyncrasies or unusual interests make them stand out from the norm. Maybe their use of language is somewhat different. Sometimes they exhibit odd behaviors or mannerisms. Teasing and bullying by typical peers can escalate. For some children, school is no longer "the safe place" it used to be. It is often at such times that self-esteem will plummet and depression will rear its head.

Example I:

Joey, a twelve-year old boy with Asperger's had some particular quirks that annoyed his peers, particularly at lunch time. Often he would chew with his mouth open, talk loudly and "get in people's faces." He was fond of wearing bow ties. Soon his peers were refusing to sit at the same lunch table as Joey. Because of his ostracism from the group, Joey resorted to sitting with a table of girls.

Very often during this time, children with autism/Asperger's syndrome begin to have an awareness that they are unique creatures and are different from many if not most of their peers. They may then begin to question their individuality.

Parents frequently ask when it is appropriate to tell their child about their diagnosis. The author feels that this is a personal choice. When the child is voicing that they are different from other children, it's probably a good idea to begin discussing their diagnosis so that they have some sort of framework for understanding their uniqueness. Emphasizing that being different is not bad and that we are all unique from one another can be helpful. Parents can explain that being unconventional can be a good thing and can then proceed to describe individuals from history that have made their mark because of their uniqueness. Norm Ledgin, in his book, "Asperger's and Self Esteem,"[1] describes many famous historical figures who exhibited symptoms and characteristics of autism/Asperger's Syndrome. The gifts these individuals have brought to the world have made a wonderful impact on all of us. Such explanations can help the student to value their own individuality.

[1] Ledgin, Norm, Asperger's and Self-Esteem, Future Horizons Inc., Arlington, TX 2002.

Having good self-esteem also comes from the realization that there are things that we do good, and things that we need to improve about ourselves. It is often helpful to use a visual method of demonstrating the child's strengths and weak areas so that they can view them more concretely. Parents can help develop this visual representation with the child's input:

— What's Great About Me —	
Things I'm Exceptional at Doing:	Things I need to Work on:
Take care of my pets	Catching and throwing balls
Playing video games	Trying not to scream when I'm angry
Working on the computer	Trying not to cry when I'm upset
Math Class	Being a friend
Putting puzzles together	Keeping my room neater
Playing my trumpet	Finishing my School work

Figure 8.1

Parents can explain that everything in the "I need to work on" category can be improved with practice and help! As parents, we bear the burden of ensuring that our child has opportunities to improve weak areas both in and out of school. Identifying one or two items from the "I need to work on" category with your child will help them to feel a part of the master plan and will certainly enlist their cooperation.

While your child's social deficits are being addressed, it is important to keep an eye on their self-esteem and to avoid depression. Medication only addresses the symptoms of depression, but not its root cause. When a child begins a pharmaceutical treatment program, it is important to also put in place a plan to help address the reason for the depression. Medication, however, may provide that extra support that helps a child to begin their journey back from depression when other programs have failed. In the end, children with autism/Asperger's will need to understand that having autism/Asperger's is only one facet of the "gem" of who they really are. They will need to learn to accept this part of them and recognize that it, too, provides them with wonderful qualities and skills that other children may not have.

Here are some additional tips for building self-esteem:

- If a child has previously been rewarded for good or appropriate behavior, do not take away such rewards when they exhibit problem behaviors.[2]

- Allow the child to have as much independence as possible. If they are constantly prompted to do things or has someone who does everything for them, they will never learn to feel competent/confident. Children who are confident have good self-esteem. They are resilient to life's ups and downs.

- Always be clear as to what behaviors you approve or do not approve. Do not use words such as "You were bad at recess." Instead say, "I did not like your behavior on the playground: pushing and hitting is not allowed here."

[2]Moyes, Rebecca, "Addressing the Challenging Behavior of Children with High-Functioning Autism Syndrome in the Classroom, Jessica Kingsley Publishers, 2001, p. 70-72.

- Respond differently when your child is exhibiting incompetence vs. noncompliance.

- Find things to be proud of about your child and let them know that you feel this way. Be patient when they exhibit odd behaviors. These are symptoms of the disability. Help them to be more appropriate.

- Alert teachers to excessive teasing or bullying. Insist on "safe haven" classrooms.

- Recognize when your child may need professional help in dealing with low self-esteem.

- Be aware that often these children need to be taught how to erase negative thoughts and replace them with more positive ones. One creative mom has her child "erase" their forehead as a way of visually representing that he needs to let go of negative thoughts when they become excessive.

- Incorporate various strategies into your child's school day to deal with teasing if it is problematic.

Example I:

Dean, a fourth-grade child had difficulty with self-esteem in art education classes. Often he was awkward in this environment, and his lack of proficiency would cause him to be the brunt of jokes. Eventually, when the teasing escalated, Dean dreaded going to his art classes. His parents felt that he was slipping into depression. They tried on several occasions to discuss the problems Dean was having with the art teacher, but the teacher claimed that he wasn't noticing the teasing. Dean felt that no one was validating his feelings and began to act aggressively towards those peers who were teasing him. The parents enlisted a therapist to help Dean work through his problems in this area, and together they presented a self-evaluation form to the school district that Dean could complete with the school guidance counselor immediately after each art class. A "Comments" section was included so that Dean could identify students or situations that had bothered him in class, and this would help him to diffuse rather than fester his anger. After several forms were completed, a pattern began to emerge that centered around specific types of activities that Dean needed more practice with (cutting and coloring) and particular children that were giving him trouble. It was then that the administration stepped in, offered Dean occupational therapy once a week to address these target areas, and handled the teasing issues more proactively as well. Today, Dean is a seventh-grader. He jokes easily that art is still not his favorite class. He has come to accept that he will never be a great artist, but has joined the band and is very good at playing his instrument.

My Art Education Class

What things did we do in art class today?

_____

What things did we do that I enjoyed in class today?

_____

What things did we do today in art that I did well?

_____

What things did we do today in art that I need to work on?

_____

Are there any concerns that I would like to share?

_____

Figure 8.2

153

Children with disabilities are "protected" students under school law. When teasing and harassment prevent the student from being able to interact or participate fully in the educational experience, schools can become liable if they aren't proactive in resolving such issues.

Many school districts have developed a policy that protects children from being bullied or harassed by peers. Parents need to understand that teasing is very often an every day experience for children in the school setting. Teasing is often described as making fun of someone. Teasing, however, can be playful or mean-spirited. Often children with autism/Asperger's can not discriminate between the two and the effects of both can be harmful to their self-esteem. School staff can be instrumental here in helping children with this diagnosis to recognize and respond appropriately to teasing. When teasing moves from an occasional occurrence and takes on a more persistent quality, addressing it should also take on a new dimension, as in Dean's case in Example I above.

Bullying is a more serious form of teasing. It happens when someone is cruel and chooses a target that is at a disadvantage mentally or physically. Children should never be expected to 'put up with' bullying from peers. Parents have a right to expect their school district staff to protect their child from such behavior. It is often easy to distinguish bullying from teasing because it usually involves the child's safety and occurs in a more serious and persistent manner. Case law has provided us with examples that schools can be held accountable when staff is made aware of excessive teasing/bullying of a special needs student, and they turn a blind eye. If the student then suffers emotional or physical trauma because of school neglect, they can find themselves facing damages.

Harassment is the most severe form of teasing. It is constant, and the person administering it knows that the victim will feel threatened. It is this type of behavior that courts will often address. School districts are to provide an atmosphere appropriate for learning. When a student can not come to school and expect a safe environment where they can concentrate and learn, the school should always intervene on the students behalf.

One support that can be included in the IEP for children with autism/Asperger's is to designate a safe person at school for this student. The safe person can be available to listen to the student, validate their feelings and intervene with the problem students if necessary. The safe person should also be someone who can help the child to develop some strategies for dealing with the teasing appropriately. Meetings with the safe person can be self-initiated or be included as a regular part of the student's school day/week. If regular counseling sessions are incorporated as part of the student's school week, this needs to be written in the "Related Services" portion of the IEP. Self-initiated meetings can be done verbally (the student walks to the safe person's office or classroom) or in writing (they complete a form which is then delivered to the safe person who will come to the classroom and pull them out for private conference.)

Self-initiated services are often listed in the "Program Modifications / Specially Designed Instruction" portion of the IEP and teach the child to be responsible and proactive in seeking help. Sometimes, it is better to have a program that includes both. In this way, schools can keep maximum tabs on teasing and bullying and help students who may not be so forthcoming with their problems.

In conclusion, it is important to stress that when children begin to show signs of low self-esteem that parents and schools need to be proactive in

Request for Help with a Problem

1. What happened to upset you today?

_____

2. How upset are you? On a scale of 1 to 10, with 1 being not very upset and 10 being very upset?

_____

3. Do you want someone to talk with today about this problem or is tomorrow ok?

_____

4. Do you need someone to talk to you immediately?

_____

5. Do you feel safe in school today?

_____

(Please give this form to your classroom teacher and he/she will get someone to come speak with you privately.)

Figure 8.3

developing some strategies to help. When a child exhibits poor self-esteem, other challenging behaviors may begin to surface as the child struggles to find ways to deal with their pain. These behaviors (such as aggression, violent talk, isolation) may then be even more difficult to address. It is always easiest to address behaviors when they are at the least intrusive stage.

Chapter Nine

What to Do
with Problem
Behaviors

A student with high-functioning autism/Asperger's syndrome will often have challenging behaviors. Some of the most frequently reported are:

- Difficulty with peer relationships.

- Problems maintaining attention.

- Meltdowns/inability to manage anxiety.

- Sensory issues.

- Problems with transitions.

- Poor self-esteem/depression.

- Task avoidance or shut-down type behavior.

- Tantrums.

- Self-stimulatory/self-abusive behavior.

Many children with autism/Asperger's can benefit from a behavior support plan. This may seem to some parents to be a negative thing. Some parents may feel that aside from a few "bumps" in the road, their child's behavior is good and drawing attention to the poor behaviors is not something they want to do. Parents need to realize, though, as was stated in Chapter One, if the IEP does not specify exactly how the child's disability may manifest in the classroom, then this student, in the eyes of special education law, may be treated exactly as a typical student with regard to their problem behaviors.

Bryan, a 15-year old student with high-functioning autism attends his school district's middle school. When Bryan is teased, he often reacts violently and aggressively. He may say things that are completely inappropriate such as: "I'm going to bring my dad's gun to school tomorrow and blow your head off!" Bryan's parents brought a letter to their IEP meeting from their child's psychiatrist who felt that Bryan was lacking the social skills to deal with the teasing and was being inappropriate for that reason. The IEP team, however, did not adopt a behavior support plan to help address those social deficits, nor did they write how this particular manifestation of his disability might appear in the classroom. Bryan was suspended several times for being aggressive with peers. Finally, Bryan was expelled from school for making terroristic threats after he shouted that he was going to kill his teacher when she disciplined him for hitting a peer. Bryan tried to explain that the peer had called him an obscene name, but the teacher had not witnessed this and felt that she could not discipline the other student for something she had not seen.

Sadly, these types of incidents as described above are somewhat common among children with this disability who have behavioral issues. Families need to provide extra protections for these vulnerable children as they try to navigate the school's rough waters.

Does My Child Really Need a Behavior Support Plan?

Special education law provides two criteria for deciding if a child needs a behavior support plan. The first question that the team should ask in making this determination is: "Does this child have challenging behaviors?" The team should then ask: "Do these behaviors impact on the child's learning or the learning of others'?"

If the answer to both questions is "yes," then the student should have a behavior support plan developed. If parents are experiencing difficulty convincing the team that this is indeed the case, they should document each phone call they receive regarding their child's challenging behavioral episodes and reiterate the contents of these calls back in letter form to the teacher so there is a record of the call. (Refer to letter found in Chapter Four, Figure 4.1.)

These letters, along with any notes sent home from the child's teachers or administrators, will serve to build a case for the need to develop a behavior support plan.

How a Good Behavior Support Plan is Developed

There are two ways to collect data with intent to write a behavior support plan. The first way involves an informal-type process.

This informal collection of data usually includes information obtained from an interview with the parents and the teachers to see exactly what problem behaviors the student is having and what supports could be added to assist them. Sometimes, there is added data obtained from an observation of the child's behavior in the school setting. When the plan is developed, the information is shared via a report, and a plan is then developed which usually includes the suggestions of parents and teachers. The plan would most likely detail what consequences will be applied when the student exhibits the behaviors and what rewards will be implemented when they comply. This type of plan works well when behaviors are fairly new and of minor intensity.

When behaviors are more engrained and significant, a second way of collecting data is often more useful. This collection of information is referred to as a functional behavioral assessment. This is where the team observes the child over a longer period of time across their school day, and the data that is collected is compiled to see if there are patterns to their behaviors (i.e. they occur at a certain time of the day, in a certain academic subject area, involve similar types of activities or with certain people, etc.). The purpose of examining the data is to try to discover what function the child's behavior is serving for them or what they are trying to communicate through poor behavior. When a functional behavior assessment is completed, all team members have a chance to offer their input. The team looks for the reasons why the behavior is occurring so that interventions can be planned to address the assumed deficits that cause the student to respond in a poor manner. A hypothesis as to why the behavior is occurring is then developed, and a list of supports are put in place to help prevent the problem behavior. The team also sits down and addresses the hierarchy of consequences that will be tried when the behavior is displayed, along with a reward system to reinforce appropriate behavior.

The list of typical challenging behaviors in children with autism/Asperger's provided at the beginning of this chapter can serve as a good guideline for deciding what supports the student will need in his/her behavior support plan. For instance, if a student is having difficulty managing stress, what things can we put in place to help them so that they don't have melt-downs? What exactly is causing the stress? Is it too much sensory overload? Is the work too hard? Should we test to make sure that their reading/math level are appropriate for the work they are expected to do? Are there too many transitions during the school day that are upsetting?

Parents have wonderful input to share about their children, and their ideas and suggestions can often be extremely beneficial:

Example II:

Peter would frequently react to loud noises. Often he would scream, throw himself on the ground and attempt to block out the noise by covering his ears. His teacher noticed that Peter was frequently covering his ears in her classroom. Peter's parents observed the classroom and felt that the noise level was too loud for him at times. The classroom was fairly unstructured, and the kids were required to move to different stations in the room and encouraged to interact with one another to finish the work of each station. Although Peter's parents felt that the teacher had an extraordinary classroom with plenty of opportunities to discover and learn through many multi-sensory activities, they felt that Peter needed a more structured environment. The team decided to move Peter to a new classroom that would better suit his needs.

Example III:

Marty was a kindergarten student who frequently had meltdowns and occasionally refused to do classroom assignments. After the functional behavior assessment was completed, a pattern of work-refusal became evident that included mostly tasks involving coloring, cutting and pasting. It was also determined through parent and teacher input that Marty's fine motor skills were very delayed. The team then met to develop Marty's behavioral support plan. It was *agreed that Marty would need to receive occupational therapy. The team also decided that Marty's teacher should modify these types of tasks down to Marty's level of performance. He would also receive reinforcement if he attempted the work, and even more reinforcement through a special reward system if he completed all parts of the task.*

Identifying the Missing Skill to be Taught

Once the hypothesis is determined as to why the student is having so many difficulties, the team can then begin to focus on identifying various skills that need to be taught. These are often termed "replacement behaviors." For instance, if a student is having trouble managing their anxiety, then one possible replacement behavior would be for the student to learn to recognize the signals their body gives them when they are stressed and identify how stressed they actually are (see Chapter Seven, Figure 7.3). Another replacement behavior would be to teach the student what to do to relieve their stress when they identify that they are mildly anxious versus severely anxious.

Antecedent Strategies

Antecedent strategies are those strategies that are put in place to help prevent problem behavior. They are the supports that the child needs to address their deficits.

Example IV:

David was a third-grade student who also had many meltdowns during his school day. It was determined through David's functional behavior assessment that the hypothesis for David's behavior was that he was having difficulty with transitions both in and out of the classroom. In the classroom, he would refuse to move on to the next activity or act as if he was deaf when it was announced that it was time to begin a new activity. When it was time to move to another classroom for a new activity, David would sometimes become aggressive with peers while waiting in line or leave the line and run off. The team developed many antecedent strategies for this hypothesis. They developed a picture schedule and reviewed it with him at the start of the school day and frequently throughout the day. They created picture transition cards (see figure 9.2) and would provide those to David several minutes before it was time to move to an activity outside the classroom. The teacher incorporated five-minute warnings between various activities in her classroom so that David would know that a new activity was about to begin. David's behaviors decreased significantly once the supports were in place.

Transition Cue Card

Figure 9.1

Consequential Strategies

Strategies that are put in place for staff to do after the behavior occurs are called consequences. Consequences do not have to be negative in nature.

Example V:

Alicia had trouble modulating her voice. She would often speak very loudly. A consequential strategy was used in the form of a visual cue card resembling the volume knob of a radio to teach Alicia where the volume of her voice should be. When Alicia was speaking loudly, the teacher would visually show her where she was on the volume and where her voice needed to be. Alicia was able to modulate her voice at once.

In the book, Addressing the Challenging Behavior of Children with High Functioning Autism/Asperger's Syndrome in the Classroom,[1] the author lists several types of consequential strategies that can be positive in nature; that

[1]Moyes, Rebecca, Addressing the Challenging Behavior of Children with High Functioning Autism/Asperger's Syndrome in the Classroom, Jessica Kingsley Publishers, 2002, p. 119.

is, they serve to teach or reinforce appropriate behavior, rather than to punish. They include:

- Having the student issue an apology with an explanation of what they did wrong.

- Having the student explain, write, or draw the depiction of what they did wrong.

- Reviewing with the student the rule book or rule chart.

- Reviewing with the student or developing with the student a social story that explains the problem behavior.

- Having the student make up for poor behavior: if they did something unkind to another student, then they would have to do something nice for them.

As stated earlier in this chapter, consequences should be arranged in the form of a hierarchy from least intrusive to most intrusive. For instance, if a student exhibits the negative behavior one time during the school day, the consequence should be different than if they exhibit it five times during the same day.

Rewards/Motivators

Elisa Gagnon, in her book, Power Cards: Using Special Interests to Motivate Children and Youth with Asperger's Syndrome and Autism,[2] writes that special interests or "passions" can be tremendous motivators for students with autism spectrum disorders. Passions can be used as rewards or as creative ways to encourage on-task behaviors:

---

[2]Gagnon, Elisa, Power Cards: Using Special Interests to Motivate Children and Youth with Asperger's Syndrome and Autism, Autism/Asperger Publishing Company, 2001. 104.

Example VI:

Christian was a 14-year old boy who enjoyed anything having to do with the Statute of Liberty. In fact, Christian often expresses that when he is an adult, he would like to be employed in some manner on Staten Island, NY. Christian can tell you how many steps there are from the entrance doorway of the Statute to her crown. He can tell you what the seven stars in Lady Liberty's crown represent. In school, one of his most difficult classes was art. He would exhibit work refusal and be disruptive almost every period he had art. Nothing appeared to be helping the situation until his teacher, on the advice of Christian's mother, developed a reward system that if Christian complied with directives, remained on task and was nondisruptive during class, he would earn a picture of the Statute of Liberty. There was an immediate change in his behavior.

Summary

For students with autism and autism/Asperger's syndrome, developing an appropriate behavior support plan can be an important tool in maintaining inclusion in regular education classrooms and least restrictive placements Often it will be necessary to revise and revisit the plans to add additional supports or address new problem areas as they surface. Consequences and reward systems may need to be re-worked to reflect changing interests and/or effectiveness. Behavior support plans are not designed to merely manage behaviors or make them disappear. They are designed to address skill deficits and provide supports to help children learn to achieve the skills they might be lacking.

Chapter Ten

What to Do When the Team Can Not Agree

As an educational advocate for this population, the author has often been posed this question many times from parents. They say that they have tried everything they can, but they feel as if they are on the losing side of the table. They see the individualized education program (IEP) as a document that will ensure their child's success in the educational setting, and they want it worded just right. Yes, it's personal for them: their child's life is at stake! They know the supports their child needs, and yet, they just can't convince the district to provide them. They often feel as if they are hammering out a contract. They have difficulty understanding why professionals in education would not want to teach their child in the manner that is needed.

First, the author tries to explain to parents that it's not a matter of winning or losing. If you feel that you are winning, it's probably because you think that the IEP is a workable document for your child and provides them with all the services they will need. If you feel that you are losing, it's probably because you haven't achieved all that you wanted for them, or you see that they are not making progress. Remember that the team helped to select those supports. You can always go back to the team at any time and say, "This isn't working. You have informed me time after time that my child's behavior is not appropriate." Or:

"You have informed me that his/her grades are not improving, and he/she is not making progress on some of his/her goals." Or: "My child is regressing. He/she doesn't want to come to school. He/she has no friends." You can also go to the meeting and say, "When we developed this document, you felt that a few of the supports I asked for were not necessary. You felt that this document was sufficient, and I agreed to give it a try. Now, we need to consider adding additional supports." The data that you have collected as explained in previous chapters will be the key to unlocking that IEP door.

The IEP is a contract: but it is a contract for services, not for performance. The IEP is not a guarantee that your child will perform at a predetermined level. If you feel that your child is not performing at their best this could be because the document is inadequate, you will need to convince the team. Private evaluations are critical-professionals in the education field who can offer their opinions that support your arguments can be invaluable. If the district is providing for the services they agreed to do in the IEP, they are in compliance. They are fulfilling their part of the contract.

The Individuals with Disabilities Education Act (IDEA)

Under IDEA (the Individuals with Disabilities Education Act that governs special education law), school districts obtain funds from their federal and state governments to provide special education services to special needs children. These funds may or may not be enough to cover the cost of all supports and programs that these children need. Consequently, local tax dollars are also earmarked for these programs. Those individuals at your meetings that often provide you with the most resistance are usually the "gatekeepers" at the IEP table. They need to make budget-conscious decisions when deciding which children get what services. It's not a fair system; but, unfortunately, that's the system our federal government has adopted. Until this process is changed, designing programs for special education students will always involve a consideration of how much they cost. Parents can play active roles in changing policy by lobbying their congressmen if they feel that budgeting is constantly controlling whether or not their children get needed programs.

Begin With Your IEP Team Members

As a parent, when you feel that you have reached an impasse, you do have several options. The author does recommend that you speak with your child's teacher first. Schedule a phone or in-person visit to try to work things out at this level or gain his/her support. Your child's teacher knows how their student is performing in the classroom and if the services offered are enough. You can also request that the IEP team reconvene.

Bring an Advocate

Getting an advocate involved may help for several reasons. Educational advocates have knowledge of special education law. Often they can tell you if you are asking for something the school district will not be able to do due to certain special education regulations. They can also inform you of ways to get what you feel your child is entitled to get. Advocates help parents to feel that 'someone is on their side' and provide support when meetings turn sour. Many advocates are trained in conflict resolution. For this reason, they can be assets at meetings. When parents get emotionally involved, it is sometimes difficult to stay focused and take notes. Advocates can serve this role as well. Many times, after working with other parents who have children with similar issues, advocates can bring to the table valuable suggestions for helping to resolve problem areas.

The author believes that the advocate should not speak for the parent. Many parents feel that when an advocate is present, they can sit back and relax and let him/her do the talking. This should never be the case. Advocates can and should, however, lend support either through questions or comments that might clarify what the parent is trying to achieve and navigate sticky points of concern for both sides.

Ask for Mediation

Federal law also requires that school districts must ensure that a mediation process be available should the parent desire to take advantage of it when districts request a hearing to change a child's placement or program. The mediation should be conducted by a 'qualified and impartial hearing officer who is trained in effective mediation techniques.'[1] Often the Bureau of Special

---

[1]Part 300, "Individuals with Disabilities Education Act," Federal regulations, section 300.506, "Mediation."

Education in your state will select the mediator at random. If not, both parties should agree to the selection of this individual. Discussions in mediation are confidential and whatever is agreed to in this meeting will be incorporated into a written mediation agreement. If a parent or school district still feels that the agreement reached in mediation is not sufficient, either has the right to request a due process hearing. The details of the mediation may not be used in this hearing. Generally, parents can not request mediation more than one time in a school year and/or for the same issue. The mediation process is a free service.

Ask for a Prehearing Conference

This option is not available in all states but is a very valuable way to avoid the costs associated with a due process hearing as it often serves as a valuable step in resolving conflict. Many times, parents and schools will bring their attorneys, but this is not always the case. Generally, if the parents bring an attorney, so will the district. In reality, a prehearing conference is nothing more than a more formal IEP conference. Prehearing conferences work best when the parties agree to focus their discussion on the points of dissent that they have about the IEP.

There is no limit to the number of prehearing conferences that can be held. As long as both parties agree to continue meeting in this manner and feel that the team is making progress, this can be a viable process for resolving conflict.

Impartial Due Process Hearing

A parent or a public agency (school district) can initiate a hearing on any of the matters relating to the 'identification, evaluation or educational placement of a child with a disability, or the provision of a free and appropriate education to the child.'[2] The hearing officer must be impartial and must not have a conflict of interest with either the school district or the parent. It is advised that parents hire an attorney to represent their child as the hearing resembles a court case; i.e., there will be presentation of evidence and examining and cross-examining of witnesses. If either the school district or the parents are not happy with the decision of the hearing officer, they can appeal their case to the State Education Agency (SEA). The official conducting the case at the SEA level will review the entire hearing record, may provide the opportunity to listen to or read additional testimony or seek other evidence. Once the decision is made at the SEA level,

---

[2]Part 300, "Individuals with Disabilities Education Act," Federal regulations, section 300.507, "Impartial Due Process Hearing; Parent Notice."

either side can also appeal in a civil action in a state court or in a district federal court.

Due process hearings can be extremely expensive, often approaching $10,000 or more. More importantly, they usually sever any remaining relationship the parents have with the district. There are emotional costs as well: the stress and strain on marriages and the anxiety involved in preparing a case can be tremendous. The following are some actual parent comments about due process:

Example I:

'We have big debts. You should see the bills. We've run over $14,000 in debt on this thing, so we can't stop now. We have so much invested. If there was a chance that I was wrong, I would stop. But I know I'm right. We've been to every specialist from here to Rhode Island and they all say the same thing.'[3]

---

[3]Budoff, Milton, and Orenstein, Alan, Due Process in Special Education-On Going to a Hearing, the Ware Press, 1982, p. 139.

Example II:

'My husband decided that we've just had enough. We gone through two of these things. Each one is wrenching. We have been insulted and browbeaten by [school district special education director]. I would never put my child back into any school that he had anything to do with. I have given up on this so-called due process. In fact, I've advised parents to stay away from it if they can.'[4]

Example III:

'This year it came up again, and I could have gotten my ducks in a row and taken them to a hearing again. I decided not to do it . . . my hands right now are shaking as I'm talking to you about it. I'm old and I get that same horrible feeling all over. Maybe if I had been a different kind of person, but I feel it is a very difficult thing to sit across from someone and have them lie blatantly and not be able to say anything about it.'[5]

[4]Budoff, Milton, and Orenstein, Alan, Due Process in Special Education-On Going to a Hearing, the Ware Press, 1982, p. 144.

[5]Budoff, Milton, and Orenstein, Alan, Due Process in Special Education-On Going to a Hearing, Ware Press, 1982, p. 144.

But, there are also parents who have good things to report about using the due process procedure:

Example IV:

'We've been delighted with their change since the hearing. They visited the private school program and sat down with us and said, "Yes, this is what he needs now and we can't offer you similar services." They have been very cooperative.'[6]

The author recommends that parents try to avoid, at all costs, a due process hearing. As Budoff and Orenstein quote in their book, Due Process in Special Education-On Going to a Hearing, "There is also a residue of bitterness in these disputes which makes it less likely that future negotiations regarding new programs will succeed."[7]

---

[6]Budoff, Milton, and Orenstein, Alan, Due Process in Special Education-On Going to a Hearing, Ware Press, 1982, p. 145.

[7]Budoff, Milton, and Orenstein, Alan, Due Process in Special Education-On Going to a Hearing, Ware Press, 1982, p. 143.

And in the Meantime?

Parents should remember that while any of the above is occurring, pendancy applies to their child's IEP. This means that the IEP is in a "stay put" mode. All services and programs that are part of the IEP must remain in place until a decision has been reached.

What if the School District Refuses to Do or is Not Doing What Was Agreed to in the IEP?

An option exists for families in the above circumstance. Many states have a free- of-charge complaint process where a compliance officer will review the parent's complaints and offer a remedy if the district is found out of compliance. Usually, the district is ordered to comply with the IEP since they agreed to it in the first place. In some instances, compensatory time is ordered for the student if he/she was entitled to a service, and the service was not provided over a certain period of time. Sometimes, compliance officers order tutoring services for the student to make up for lost instructional time. In all cases, the compliance officer reviews your written summary of the issue, may speak with you on the phone, visits or speaks to school district representatives and issues a summary report with his/her conclusions. Generally speaking, it is looked upon more favorably if parents can list all the avenues they have taken to ask the school district to comply with the IEP and provide written documentation of such. But, this is not necessary. It should be noted that complaints that are backed with written documentation are more likely to be found in favor of the parent. Otherwise, the district will be able to provide their "side" to the matter and the compliance officer will render the complaint unfounded. It is always advisable to seek an advocate's assistance before filing a complaint.

CONCLUSION

The author would like to offer the reader one piece of advice in the form of a well-known phrase: "Pick your battles." You will have to work with your school district for many years to come. Many of the individuals you work with in IEP meetings will often be present at future IEP meetings as well. Every parent can probably list one or two things in the IEP that they are not happy with. Ask yourself whether or not those one or two things make a critical difference in your child's educational performance. This should help you decide if "you are picking the right battle." Do everything you can to keep a good working relationship with your district. On the flip side, the author also needs to state that she has seen cases where she has advised parents to file complaints and/or exercise due process because the school district absolutely refuses to work as a team or to ensure that the student with a disability receives a free and appropriate education.

Your relationship with your school district is like a marriage. It involves give and take. Sometimes there will be times when you have to give. And sometimes, there will be times when you are entitled to take, always for the sake of your child.